Theatre Appreciation

2nd Edition

Contributors

John W. James

Kenneth H. Erickson Jr.

Dean Anthony

Craig M. Smith

N. James Thaggard

© 2014

Studio 84 Productions

State College of Florida

Manatee – Sarasota

Photo Credits:

Front Cover: Studio 84 Productions at Manatee Community College presented *The Servant of Two Masters* as its inaugural production in David S. and Anne V. Howard Studio Theatre.

Back Cover (Top): Cast members of *The Servant of Two Masters* (pictured left to right): Jenna Gagliano, Joshua Fishbein, Mariana Rocha, Michael Hesemann, Michael Jorgensen, Katelyn Studer, Dayton Sinkia, Rae Crider and Carl MacMichael

Back Cover (Bottom): Cast members of *Design For Murder* (pictured left to right): Katelyn Studer, Brittany Miller, Mariana Rocha, Jenna Gagliano, Michael Jorgensen, Megan Kroger and Rachael Bayor

All photos © 2008, 2009 by Tom Oostveen and used with permission

Cover designed by Erin Erickson Saladino

Layout designed by James Thaggard

This book uses the type font TAHOMA, a sans-serif typeface designed that is nearly identical to Verdana but with tighter letter-spacing.

Maps and Timelines designed by Dean Anthony

Drawings created by Kenneth Erickson

Printed in the United States of America
ISBN: 978-0-615-30441-0

Studio 84 Productions
State College of Florida
5840 26th Street West
Bradenton, FL 34207

Dean Anthony   (941) 752-5249
Craig Smith   (941) 752-5586

www.scf.edu/theatre

TABLE OF CONTENTS

TABLE OF CONTENTS (continued)

This workbook, containing notes and readings, was designed to be used in a basic theatre appreciation class. It begins with observations regarding the current state of the art in the United States, then gives an historical perspective on Western Theatre.

Two 20th century works by American playwrights are examined in detail. **"All My Sons"** by Arthur Miller and **"A Raisin in the Sun"** by Lorraine Hansberry speak to issues that are both American and international. Another play with social and political overtones, **"Master Harold and the Boys"** by South African playwright Athol Fugard, is also viewed in this class.

The historical overview that follows includes details of classical (Greek and Roman) theatre, the Medieval and Renaissance periods, and the Elizabethan era. The term concludes with the Restoration and the Baroque periods in 17th century England. Plays read during this portion of the course include **"Antigone"** by Sophocles and **"A Midsummer Night's Dream"** by William Shakespeare. Copies of both of these scripts are included in this textbook.

As of 2014, the contributors have spent a combined total of 95 years working with freshman and sophomore students at open-door schools. We have found that students who have completed the course with this format have been consistently successful at upper division schools.

John W. James (contributor)
Kenneth H. Erickson (contributor)
Dean Anthony (contributor)
Craig M. Smith (contributor)
N. James Thaggard (contributor/editor)

THEATRE AS AN ART FORM

THEATRE DOES NOT TRANSCEND LANGUAGE.
You must understand the language to fully understand the play.
(Understanding the language does not guarantee understanding the play.)

FOUR ELEMENTS THAT DISTINGUISH THEATRE FROM OTHER ART FORMS

1. **Theatre is TEMPORAL** - Each performance is a distinct work of art. (No two performances are ever exactly the same.)

2. **Theatre is MIMETIC** - It Recreates, Reproduces or Represents (Most of the time a song is a song. It does not try to recreate, reproduce or represent something else. A play on the other hand always does.)

3. **Theatre is INTERPRETIVE** - From one production to the next, the only thing that remains constant is the script. For each production, the script and all aspects of the production are interpreted by the various artists. We don't talk so much about HAMLET as we talk about someone's *interpretation* of HAMLET.

4. **Theatre is SYNTHESIS** - It is a combination of art forms and a collaboration of artists. It is the most collaborative of all the arts.

(WILLING) SUSPENSION OF DISBELIEF
Allowing ourselves to be lied to; setting aside our knowledge that what we are viewing is not real, and temporarily accepting it as real.

In regards to art you often hear someone say:
"I know what I like"
"I just want to get my money's worth."

There is a larger truth if they are slightly altered:
"I like what I know."
"I get more for my money when I know why I have (or have not) gotten my money's worth."

Most likely, it is not nearly as important to you, as an individual, to have liked or disliked a piece of art as it is for you, an educated person, to understand why you did or did not enjoy the piece, and to also understand why others feel the way they do about the piece.

Audiences can be categorized into three broad categories:
the Escapists, the Moralists and the Artsakists.
(Please keep in mind that these are extremes, and that most theatre-goers are some mixture of the three.)

Escapists: These people want to forget the worries and cares of everyday life. They desire only to be amused and choose to see lighter plays and musicals. This audience type can be found in all walks of life and despite the lack of intellectual depth in their choices, they are often highly intelligent people. This is perhaps the largest of the three groups, and the group for which most commercial theatre is done.

Moralists: These people want to only see shows that are uplifting, teach valuable lessons or advocate parts of life of which they personally approve. They close their minds to anything outside of their (narrow) scope and demand that only "nice clean" plays be presented. This audience type is found everywhere and is one of the most serious concerns a non-commercial theatre director must deal with. (Nearly all educational theatre, is non-commercial.) This group refuses to see theatre as a reflection of life, or that life is not always "nice and clean." They refuse to see life as it really is. In either case, the Moralists' criticism of the theatre that they disagree with is not fairly delivered.

Artsakists: This is a made-up term for theatergoers whose chief concern is "art for art's sake." They have great scorn for box-office successes. They believe theatre should not be for the masses (for Escapists); rather, it should belong to them, the self-professed intellectuals. This group arrogantly concludes that popularity with a mass audience is a sure sign of mediocrity, and that only someone less than a true artist would seek it out.

The obligation of the audience:
1. To view each play from beginning to end with a sufficient imaginary energy
2. To recognize their own personal predispositions
3. To discern and appraise all the artists who have made the play possible
4. To allow each artist the right to express himself as he or she sees fit
5. To always ask Johan Wolfgang von Goethe's three questions:

        What is the artist trying to do?

        How well has he or she done it?

        Is it worth doing?

THE WORK OF MAKING A PLAY

THE CRAFTSWORKERS

PLAYWRIGHTING: the creation of the script. This craft is usually done away from the theatre building itself, and can often take place centuries and/or continents away from the current production.

ACTING: actors perform the various characters in a play.

DESIGNING: numerous designers of scenery, costumes, lighting, sound, properties, wigs, as well as programs and advertising, combine to create all of the audio and visual elements of a production

BUILDING: crafts workers execute the creative designs into reality. These include carpenters, painters, electricians, sound and recording engineers, costumers, seamstresses, wigmakers/stylists, makeup artists and others.

RUNNING: technicians properly and efficiently "run" a show with lighting and sound cues, scenery shifting, properties placement and launder and repair costumes; on occasion special effects personnel and costume dressers are also required.

THE MANAGERS

PRODUCING: person (or persons) who secure all of the necessary financing; personnel, and rehearsal and performance spaces; supervise all production and promotional aspects; address all legal matters.

DIRECTION: person (or persons) who control and develop the play with a unified vision, coordinate all of the components, and supervise all rehearsals.

STAGE MANAGING: person (or persons) who "run" the production of the play in all areas for every performance.

HOUSE MANAGING: person (or persons) who oversee the comfort of the audience and coordinate a staff of ushers who handle the admission of the audience by assisting with ticket collecting and seating.

BOX OFFICE: person (or persons) who are responsible for the ordering, organization and sale of tickets, as well as the collection and reconciliation of monies and receipts.

Depending on the size of the theatre staff and union restrictions (if they apply), these jobs may overlap with some artists performing more than one job.

Greek playwrights wrote, directed and designed their plays, and often performed in them as well.

In modern theatres, playwrights may direct, directors may also act, designers may also build, and builders may also run.

TYPES OF SCENERY

WINGED SET: Composed of wing, drop, and borders, backdrop or cyc.

DRAPED SET: The entire acting area is surrounded with drapery used as borders, legs, and traverse curtains, and may be used in conjunction with set pieces.

BOX SET: The walls on three sides are filled in solidly with flats of some kind with a framed ceiling.

PORTAL SET: Originally, there were two permanent side doors or arches, one on each side of the downstage areas and were used widely in early theatres. These doors were once referred to as "Shakespeares" and disappeared in the 19th century. In modern theatre, the portal set has the same downstage doors throughout the play, and is altered by a change of the rear wall flats and upstage side-wall flats.

PERMANENT, SKELETAL, or MULTIPLE SET: Used in multi-scene shows. It can consist of permanent flats and the insertion of additional pieces (doorframes, fireplace, window, or furniture) to change the locale.

UNIT SET: Similar to a permanent set in that most flats remain throughout the performance. The change is made by rearranging the flats and set pieces or adding new pieces and "striking" others.

SLIDING, WAGON, STAGE SET: A low platform mounted on rollers, running on tracks, as wide as the proscenium opening, and large enough to contain an entire set. While one sliding wagon is onstage, an offstage wagon may be set for a quick scene change.

REVOLVING SET: A large circular disc constructed with swivel castors, moved electronically or propelled by a windlass below so that the circular unit may revolve. The scenery is placed in such a way that as one set is moving out of sight, another is being revealed.

PROJECTED SET: Usually projected from the rear and used as a substitute for painted backdrops and background decor needed for suggestive or space staging. Various types of projectors are used.

SIMULTANEOUS SETTING: Everything required by the technical demands of the play is onstage. Its beginnings can be traced to the Middle Ages, when a general playing space, or platea, was used to represent particular locales.

TYPES OF STAGES

PROSCENIUM: Box-like, enclosed, the fourth-wall is revealed and can be curtain-controlled.

THREE-QUARTER THRUST: Stage juts out into the audience area creating a "U" or horseshoe shape.

ARENA: Stage is a circular platform and the audience completely surrounds it. Also referred to as Theatre-in-the-Round.

ENVIRONMENTAL: Similar to arena stage, but the performing area is usually a small square-shape, and the audience sits on multiple levels as high as twenty feet above the playing area.

AMPHITHEATRE: Large oval or semi-circular outdoor theatre with tiers of seats surrounding the open playing area. Also, a very large indoor auditorium.

FOUND: Any converted structure not originally built to house theatrical productions.

FOUR ELEMENTS OF DRAMA:

EXPOSITION: The part of the play that explains who the characters are, where and when they exist, and important events that happened before the play begins. This is usually done through dialogue and often establishes what problem must be solved.

COMPLICATION: The element of a play that develops through a series of crises. Each crisis demands a decision, which sets up for a new situation moving to another crisis.

CLIMAX: The highest emotional point for the audience and/or the major turning point for the characters that usually occurs late in the play.

RESOLUTION: The element of a play that usually happens shortly after the climax when all or most of the problems have been brought to some type of conclusion.

FOUR POINTS THAT OFTEN DETERMINE THE SUCCESS OR FAILURE OF A PLAY:

STORY: The complete narrative of all of the events on which the play is based. The "story" of *Hamlet* must include the poisoning of Hamlet's father, but since Shakespeare omitted this scene in his play, the poisoning is considered part of the story (learned through "exposition") rather than part of the "plot".

PLOT: The order and arrangement of events and characters in a play. The part of the story that is dramatized <u>during</u> the course of the play.

CHARACTERS: The persons created by the playwright who can best carry out the theme and plot of the play, usually through speeches and actions.

The central character in a play is called the **protagonist** (from the Greek "protagonistes", the first actor). The individual, thing, or force opposing the protagonist is called the **antagonist** (from the Greek "antagonistes", the competitor or rival.)

THEME: The central idea which the playwright wants to communicate to the audience. The theme is the fundamental idea of what a play is about. A theme can usually be stated in one or two abstract words and the playwright makes this abstract concept concrete though plot and characterization. The theme of Arthur Miller's *Death of a Salesman* could be stated as "human dignity", while the theme of Eugene O'Neill's *Desire Under the Elms* could be stated as "lust".

REQUIREMENTS OF A TRADITIONAL GREEK TRAGEDY

1. The play must contain a serious subject.
2. The protagonist must be a great figure of heroic proportions. He must represent more than one individual.
3. The incidents must be absolutely honest and without the element of chance. What should happen must happen.
4. The basic emotions are those of pity and fear: pity for the protagonist's suffering and fear that the same thing might happen to us.
5. In the final analysis, the protagonist must meet defeat, but out of that defeat must come enlightenment.

Note: In modern tragedies, the protagonist may be a common, ordinary person.

REQUIREMENTS OF A MELODRAMA

1. The play must contain a serious subject.
2. Characters are more loosely drawn than in tragedy and this makes it easier for the audience to identify with the characters, thus creating a stronger emphatic response.
3. Whereas tragedy must be absolutely honest, the elements of chance and coincidence enter into melodrama.
4. There may be an emotion of pity, but it borders on sentimentality. Fear may be evident, but it is of a more temporary or surface type.
5. There is no real enlightenment even in defeat. In most instances the protagonist does win his battle.

REQUIREMENTS OF A COMEDY

1. The play treats its subject in a lighter vein, even though the subject may be a serious one.
2. The play provokes thoughtful laughter.
3. The events are both possible and probable.
4. The plot grows out of the characters rather than the situation.
5. The story is honest in its portrayal of life.

Sub-genres include:

BLACK COMEDY makes light of serious subject matters such as war *(the film-version of M*A*S*H)*, crime (*Pulp Fiction*), violence *(Fight Club)*, or religion *(Monty Python's The Life of Brian)*.

PARODY humorously imitates a serious genre such as the King Arthur legend in *Monty Python and the Holy Grail* or 1930's horror films in Mel Brooks' *Young Frankenstein*. Both of these examples were successful film parodies from the 1970's that were adapted recently as Broadway musicals.

SATIRE ridicules human behavior such as in Moliere's *Tartuffe* (religious hypocrisy); Shaw's *Arms and the Man* (glorification of war) and Wilde's *The Importance of Being Earnest* (the British upper class).

REQUIREMENTS OF A FARCE

1. The play has as its object riotous laughter and escape.
2. It asks the audience to accept certain improbabilities, but from that point on proceeds in a lifelike manner.
3. Is possible, but not very probable.
4. Is dominated by situation rather than character and calls for little or no thought.
5. It must move very rapidly in an episodic manner and is believable only for the moment.

DRAMATIC AND ARTISTIC CRITICISM

THE CRITIC (1963)   Written and narrated by Mel Brooks
                    Won Academy Award for Best Animated Film

WALTER KERR ON THEATRE (1970)

A.	NO PLACE TO BE SOMEBODY	(1969) by Charles Gordone (1930-1996) Pulitzer Prize Winning Play
B.	SHERLOCK JR.	(1924) film by Buster Keaton (1895-1966) Recent examples: THE PURPLE ROSE OF CAIRO (1985) by Woody Allen and THE LAST ACTION HERO (1995)
C.	PROMETHEUS	(c. 457 B.C.) by Aeschylus (c. 525-456 B.C.E.) Contemporary example: WHOSE LIFE IS IT ANYWAY? (1979) by Brian Clark Film version starred Richard Dreyfuss (1982)
D.	THE SERPENT	(1968) by Jean Claude Van Itallie (1936 -) The Cain and Abel scene.
E.	THE IMPORTANCE OF BEING EARNEST	(1895) by Oscar Wilde (1854-1900) How the audience affects the actor, and helps to shape performance.
F.	RICHARD III	(ca. 1593) by William Shakespeare (1564-1616) Elizabeth, Henry IV's wife, meets Richard at her husband's funeral.

The film features Philip Bosco (1930 -), one of Broadway's finest actors. He has been nominated for several Tony Awards, winning Best Actor in a Play in 1989 for LEND ME A TENOR.

WALTER KERR (1913-1996) The Leading American Drama Critic. He was married to Jean Kerr (1926-2003), a popular playwright whose plays include MARY, MARY (1954) and LUNCH HOUR (1983).

CENSORSHIP

A. RELIGIOUS
1. Leaders of religious groups
2. The entire denomination

B. PEER PRESSURE
1. Friends
2. Professional critics

C. GOVERNMENTAL
1. Elected Officials
2. Groups in Government

On February 24, 1983, John Spano, speaking for the U. S. Justice Department, said that "three documentaries by the National Film Board of Canada—two on acid rain and an anti-war film nominated for an Academy Award—have been ruled 'political propaganda', and must be labeled as such for showing in this country, as the work of registered foreign agents."

Hundreds, if not thousands, of foreign films are shown annually in this country. Only about 25% are screened for propaganda content and only about half of those are required to carry the label that they are the work of registered foreign agents.

The anti-war film, IF YOU LOVE THIS PLANET, subsequently won the Academy Award. Many Americans never saw the film because many film exhibitors were frightened by the "foreign agents" label. The other two films, ACID FROM HEAVEN and ACID RAIN: REQUIEM OR RECOVERY?, expressed the opinion that acid rain is an *American* problem. The Justice Department took exception to that perspective and gave the films the "propaganda" and "work of foreign agents" labels.

The USIA (United States Information Office) could keep films from being exported.

THEATRE ETIQUETTE

Attending a live theatre performance is a very different experience than watching television at home or going out to the movies. Here are some tips of what is expected of theatre audience members.

Before you arrive at the theatre:

Prepare for your theatre experience by learning about the playwright and perhaps the time period in which the play takes place.

If possible, buy a ticket prior to the show to avoid disappointment of a sold-out performance. Note that tickets are sold for a specific date and time and usually for a specific seat. Be sure to check your ticket when you buy it because often tickets are neither refundable nor exchangeable. The time listed on your ticket is the time that the show actually starts. Remember, there are no previews of coming attractions at a live theatre performance!

Plan to arrive 15-30 minutes early to find your seat and to read your program. Studio 84 Productions at SCF does not seat any latecomers once the show begins as latecomers disturb the performance for the actors and other audience members.

Use the water fountain and restroom before the show starts. Audience members should not leave or enter the theatre during the show unless there is an emergency.

Be sure to eat before or after the show—never during a show! No food or drink is allowed in the SCF theatres. If needed, cough drops or lozenges should be unwrapped before the show begins.

When you arrive at the theatre:

An usher will welcome you to the performance and ask for your ticket. At most SCF theatre productions your ticket will have a specific row and seat number. Be sure to sit in your assigned seat so that you don't cause confusion for other audience members.

Turn off your cell phone, beeper and other electronic devices so that you do not disturb the performers and other audience members or those seated around you. Often, the audience will be reminded to turn off any devices before the show begins. It is important the devices be turned off, as most "vibrate" settings are still loud enough to disrupt a performance. Use of cellphones and text messaging during a performance is never allowed.

Recording a live theatre performance (including any photography or audio) is forbidden by U.S. Copyright law. If you're caught doing so, you will be asked to leave. Flash photography is dangerous to the performers who may be blinded by the flash.

During the performance:

Give the performers your full concentration. If you talk during the performance you will disturb the concentration of everyone around you and possibly the performers on stage. Don't miss the moment; there is no pause and rewind button in live theatre.

Watch and listen to the performance with an open mind and a relaxed body, ready to absorb every detail. It is important that you listen attentively so that you don't miss anything and so that you don't disturb others around you.

Remember that you and the actors have an agreement called "the willing suspension of disbelief." Actors will create an imaginary world in which the play takes place, and you agree to accept this imaginary world as real.

After the performance has ended:

When the play is over, show your appreciation by applauding for the performers.

At the end of the performance there is usually a curtain call. This is when the actors return to the stage to receive your appreciation. Don't leave during the curtain call. Wait until it is over and then exit with the rest of the audience.

BROADWAY and OFF-BROADWAY

By definition, a **BROADWAY** theatre is located in the Theatre District in Midtown Manhattan with a seating capacity of 500 or more. The smallest Broadway theatre is the 597-seat Helen Hayes Theatre on 44th Street; the largest is the 1933-seat George Gershwin Theatre on 51st Street. As of 2009, there were 41 Broadway theatres, most of which are owned by three groups: The Shubert Organization, the Nederlander Organization and Jujamcyn. Broadway productions use only union employees in all phases of production.

OFF-BROADWAY originally referred to a theatre located near Broadway, but is now defined as a professional venue in New York City with a seating capacity between 99 and 500, or a specific production that appears in such a venue and adheres to related trade union and other contracts. When the costs of staging Broadway plays became excessive, Off-Broadway began as a recognizable movement and allowed for experimentation and revival. Off-Broadway theatres are located everywhere in the Manhattan area, and use facilities such as warehouses, basements and churches.

Some OFF-BROADWAY plays have become successful in BROADWAY theatres, although the overwhelming majority have not. Some which transferred to BROADWAY are:

HAIR (1968)	opened in the Biltmore Theatre after performing Off-Broadway for two years. This production protested a number of social situations, most notably the war in Southeast Asia. The authors of HAIR were James Rado, Galt McDermott and Tom O'Horgan. The 2009 production won a Tony Award for Best Revival of a Musical.
OH! CALCUTTA! (1969)	was a series of sketches or short one act plays and scenes. A number of contributors, including John Lennon and Sam Shepard, allowed their work to be included. The production was conceived and staged by Kenneth Tynan, a distinguished writer and critic.
A CHORUS LINE (1975)	was produced by the New York Shakespeare Festival, also known as the Joseph Papp Public Theatre. It began as a highly experimental concept and became the longest running production in the history of Broadway. (It has since been replaced by CATS, LES MISERABLES, and THE PHANTOM OF THE OPERA, the current longest-runner.) Michael Bennett conceived, choreographed and directed the production. The authors were James Kirkwood, Nicholas Dante, Marvin Hamlisch and Edward Kleban. In 1976, the musical received the Pulitzer Prize for drama and the Tony Award for best musical.
RENT (1996)	won the 1996 Pulitzer Prize for drama and Tony Award for best musical. Jonathan Larson's rock musical retelling of the "La Boheme" story is relocated to AIDS-era East Village, New York. The ending is transformed from the opera, but the theme of love striving to endure all obstacles remains.

Other Off-Broadway shows with subsequent runs on Broadway include the Tony award-winning musicals AVENUE Q (2004), SPRING AWAKENING (2007), IN THE HEIGHTS (2008) and ONCE (2012) as well as GREY GARDENS, LITTLE SHOP OF HORRORS, and SUNDAY IN THE PARK WITH GEORGE, and such Tony award-winning plays as I AM MY OWN WIFE (2004), DOUBT (2005) as well as BRIDGE & TUNNEL and COASTAL DISTURBANCES.

More typical are productions which stay in their OFF-BROADWAY venue, such as:

THE FANTASTIKS (1959)	is the longest running play in the history of the American Theatre, playing for more than 17,000 performances during its initial run (1960-2002) at the Sullivan Street Playhouse. A 2006 revival at the Snapple Theatre Center is still running as of 2014. It was written by Tom Jones and Harvey Schmidt.

Other productions, including STOMP, BLUE MAN GROUP, and ALTAR BOYZ have run for several years in their Off-Broadway locations.

PROFESSIONAL THEATRE

Broadway	Union dominated, highest wages in the various skill areas.
Off-Broadway	Union control, but with better economic options for producers. Smaller seating area.
Regional Repertory	Union contract allowance for non-union actors. Each organization negotiates its contracts with the union. Often related to a college or university. The ASOLO (FSU) and FLORIDA STUDIO THEATRE (no college affiliation) are both in this category.
L O R T	League of Resident Theatres
Dinner Theatres	There are several professional and non-professional dinner theatres across the country. Sarasota's GOLDEN APPLE DINNER THEATRE (1974-2013) was the longest running theatre of its kind in the United States.

There are other Regional professional theatres which do not have union or college affiliation.

AMATEUR THEATRE

Community Theatre	Volunteer organization which usually only pays the director on a full-time basis.

Educational Theatre

High School	
College	In its basic function, College theatre should train students in the art and profession of theatre. Audience approval, while desirable, should be a secondary consideration.
Training Schools	Examples are THE NEIGHBORHOOD PLAYHOUSE and THE AMERICAN ACADEMY OF THE DRAMATIC ARTS.

THEATRE AWARDS

NOBEL PRIZE FOR LITERATURE
* First awarded in 1888
* The highest honor for literature. It is one of 6 Nobel Prizes awarded each year.
* Administered by Swedish Academy, the award consists of a gold medal, diploma and cash
* This award has been given to playwrights including George Bernard Shaw (1925), Luigi Pirandello
    (1934), Eugene O'Neill (1936), Samuel Beckett (1969) and Harold Pinter (2005)

THE PULITZER PRIZE FOR DRAMA
* First awarded in 1918
* Endowed by Joseph Pulitzer and administered by Columbia University
* 15 member advisory board must see plays in first year of production
* Criteria: The play must be written by an American Playwright preferably dealing with American life.
    (One exception was THE DIARY OF ANNE FRANK by Goodrich & Hockett)
* Only a few playwrights have been awarded the Pulitzer Prize for Drama more than once.
    Eugene O'Neill received 4: (BEYOND HORIZON, ANNA CHRISTIE, STRANGE INTERLUDE,
        LONG DAY'S JOURNEY INTO NIGHT)
    Robert E. Sherwood received 3: (IDIOT'S DELIGHT, ABE LINCOLN IN ILLINOIS, THERE
        SHALL BE NO NIGHT)
    Edward Albee received 3: (A DELICATE BALANCE, SEASCAPE, THREE TALL WOMEN).
    George S. Kaufman received 2: (OF THEE I SING!, YOU CAN'T TAKE IT WITH YOU)
    Thornton Wilder received 2: (OUR TOWN, SKIN OF OUR TEETH)
    Tennessee Williams received 2: (A STREETCAR NAMED DESIRE, CAT ON A HOT TIN ROOF)
    August Wilson received 2: (FENCES, THE PIANO LESSON)
* Eight musicals have won the Pulitzer Prize: George and Ira Gershwin's OF THEE I SING (1932),
    Rodgers and Hammerstein's SOUTH PACIFIC (1950), Bock & Harnick's FIORELLO! 1960),
    Frank Loesser's HOW TO SUCCEED IN BUSINESS WITHOUT REALLY TRYING (1962),
    Michael Bennett's A CHORUS LINE (1976), Sondheim and Lapine's SUNDAY IN THE PARK
    WITH GEORGE (1985), Jonathan Larson's RENT (1996), and Yorkey and Kitt's NEXT TO
    NORMAL (2010).

THE NEW YORK DRAMA CRITICS CIRCLE AWARD
* First awarded in 1936
* Set up as alternative award system for the Pulitzer Prize, whose board had outraged local critics by
    overturning its own jury's recommendations.
* Members of the New York Drama Critics Circle annually vote for the best new plays of the year.
    The New York Times critics have an on-again off-again relationship with this award.
* Awards given for both Broadway and Off-Broadway productions.
* Categories: BEST AMERICAN PLAY, BEST FOREIGN PLAY, BEST MUSICAL.
* Some examples are:

    BEST AMERICAN PLAY: 1st awarded in 1936 to Maxwell Anderson, WINTERSET; Arthur Miller,
        ALL MY SONS (1947); and Lorraine Hansberry, A RAISIN IN THE SUN (1959).

    BEST FOREIGN PLAY: 1st awarded in 1938 to Paul Vincent Carroll, SHADOW & SUBSTANCE;
        Noel Coward, BLITHE SPIRIT (1942); John Osborne, LOOK BACK IN ANGER (1958);
        Martin McDonagh, THE PILLOWMAN (2005).

    BEST MUSICAL: 1st awarded in 1945 to Richard Rodgers & Oscar Hammerstein II for
        CAROUSEL. Recent Best Musical winners that disagreed with the Tony Awards (see
        next page) include THE DROWSY CHAPERONE (2006), PASSING STRANGE (2008)
        and MATILDA THE MUSICAL (2013).

THE "TONY" AWARDS (BROADWAY AWARDS)

* Officially known as the Antoinette Perry Awards (born 1888, actress, director and producer).
* Established by the American Theatre Wing in 1947, a year after the death of Miss Perry.
* Awarded each year for "distinguished achievement" in Broadway Theatre.
* Most coveted theatre award. Voters are "peers" (theatre professionals instead of critics).
* Awards presented annually for BEST PLAY and BEST MUSICAL and often for BEST REVIVAL OF A PLAY and BEST REVIVAL OF A MUSICAL.
* Eight awards presented annually for BEST ACTOR and ACTRESS, in LEADING and FEATURED roles in a PLAY and in a MUSICAL.
* Numerous creative and technical awards are presented each year for BEST DIRECTION of a PLAY and MUSICAL, BEST SCENIC, COSTUME and LIGHTING DESIGN of a PLAY and MUSICAL, as well as BEST BOOK, BEST SCORE, BEST CHOREOGRAPHY and BEST ORCHESTRATION of a MUSICAL. Other honorary awards are also given.

Recent Tony-award winners:

	Best Play	Best Musical
2004	I AM MY OWN WIFE	AVENUE Q
2005	DOUBT	MONTY PYTHON'S SPAMALOT
2006	THE HISTORY BOYS	JERSEY BOYS
2007	THE COAST OF UTOPIA	SPRING AWAKENING
2008	AUGUST: OSAGE COUNTY	IN THE HEIGHTS
2009	GOD OF CARNAGE	BILLY ELLIOT
2010	RED	MEMPHIS
2011	WAR HORSE	THE BOOK OF MORMON
2012	CLYBOURNE PARK	ONCE
2013	VANYA & SONIA & MASHA & SPIKE	KINKY BOOTS

THE DRAMA DESK AWARDS

* Created in 1955
* Recognizes shows produced on Broadway, off-Broadway, off-off-Broadway, and legitimate not-for-profit theaters.
* Originally called the Vernon Rice Awards in honor of theater critic Vernon Rice of the New York Post, the name was changed in 1963.
* In early years, there were few categories, but now have almost identical categories as the Tonys.
* Nominations are made by theatre critics, writers and editors in various print and electronic media for theatre season May - April.
* First award for Andrew Lloyd Webber, Edward Albee, Wendy Wasserstein, George C. Scott, and Dustin Hoffman, who was offered THE GRADUATE one month after receiving the award.
*Off-Broadway productions such as DRIVING MISS DAISY and STEEL MAGNOLIAS were given greater prominence after their wins.

THE "OBIE" AWARDS (OFF-BROADWAY AWARDS)

* Established in 1956
* Recognizes "distinguished achievement in Off-Broadway and Off-Off-Broadway productions."
* Administered by New York's Village Voice newspaper.
* Honors productions in such categories as BEST PRODUCTION, BEST AMERICAN PLAY, BEST FOREIGN PLAY and BEST MUSICAL.
* Honors people in informally structured award categories such as BEST PLAYWRIGHTING, BEST DIRECTION and BEST DESIGN. Since the early 1970s awards have been given to a varying number of "DISTINGUISHED PERFORMANCES" rather than "Best Actor" and "Best Actress".
* The Obies are voted on and awarded by a panel of judges selected from their field.
* Each play eligible must be seen during the season in which it opens.

UNIONS

Unions were established to protect workers and to help guarantee fair wages and working conditions. All Broadway actors must belong to a union. Off-Broadway actors may not have to be members of a union depending on the union affiliation of the performing group.

If you are in a union, you are not allowed to take a non-union job or you will be fined and/or kicked out of the union. Some exceptions are made for special situations.

PERFORMERS/STAGE MANAGERS:

A E A   **Actors Equity Association**

As of 2014, actors appearing in a Broadway play were paid a minimum of $1,807 per week. A Broadway Stage Manager would receive a minimum of $2,551 per week for a play and $2,969 per week for a musical.

Off-Broadway actors' pay was between $400 and $700 per week, depending on the number of seats available for sale to each performance and the price of those tickets.

Actors receive additional pay for serving as an understudy, a dance captain, or performing in some other capacity.

The League of Resident Theatres (LORT) Equity contract governs employment at 96 major professional theatres (80 members of LORT and 16 independent resident theatres). Actors working in a LORT theatre range from $935 a week at the largest theatres (LORT A) to $600 at the smallest theatres (LORT D). Stage managers in these theatres receive about $100 more per week.

A E A allows for payment as low as $175 per week in small professional theatres, especially in remote regions.

Only 7% of A E A members earn an annual income of more than $40,000.

Off-Broadway Equity rates are negotiated with each Off-Broadway producer, and currently range from $566 to $1008 weekly.

S A G - A F T R A   **Screen Actors Guild - American Federation of Television and Radio Artists**

Formed in 2012, following the merger of SAG (created in 1933) and AFTRA (created in 1952), this union represents more than 160,000 film and television performers (principal and background) and radio personalities worldwide. This union for Film Actors also has minimum levels for wages, ranging from $100 to $859 per day.

A G M A   **The American Guild of Musical Artists**

This union represents 8,000 current and retired opera singers, ballet and other dancers, opera directors, backstage production personnel at opera and dance companies, and figure skaters and has its own set of salary rates.

A G V A   **The American Guild of Variety Artists**

This union represents variety entertainment, including circuses, Las Vegas showrooms and cabarets, comedy showcases, dance revues, magic shows and theme park shows. It has its own set of salary rates for magicians, jugglers, comedians, etc.

BACKSTAGE UNIONS:

I A T S E & M P M O   **The International Alliance of Theatrical Stage Employees and Moving Pictures Machine Operators**

Each local of this union establishes its own pay range.

Local #1 in New York City pays a minimum of $1,000 per week for department heads and $900 per week for assistants. Local #1 members move furniture and scenery. In other jurisdictions, the members might also help with lighting, sound and costumes.

IATSE negotiates with each Broadway producer and insiders state the actual average is $1,800 per week for department heads and $1,700 per week for assistants. The union argues that since many of the newer shows are so technically advanced that workers must have special training.

Off-Broadway IATSE payment rates are approximately the same as Broadway, but these productions do not require as many workers.

Local #412 in Sarasota has a beginning pay level of about $19 per hour for department heads and $18 per hour for general crew work.

There are other unions covering scenery construction, lighting, sound and wardrobe.

U S A   **United Scenic Artists**
                               Designers and Painters

S D C   **Stage Directors and Choreographers Society**
                               East-coast based; primarily for the legitimate stage

D G A   **Directors Guild of America**
                               West-coast based; primarily for film and television

D G   **The Dramatists Guild of America**
                               Playwrights, lyricists, composers, librettists

THEATRE CRITICAL REVIEW FORMAT AND INSTRUCTIONS

Critical reviews should be written in narrative prose. Do not use numbered or lettered paragraph breaks nor bullet lists.

Begin with an introduction which consists of the title of the play you saw as well as the playwright's name. Include where you saw the performance, the date and curtain time as well as the cost of tickets.

Next summarize the production by stating the goal of the play including your thoughts of whether the production achieved its goal. You should briefly state your impression of the play and why you have that impression. This would be similar to a thesis statement which you can go further in depth with in the body of the critique.

In the body of the critique you should start out by discussing the plot briefly and how it relates to the goal of the production. Here you can describe when and where the play takes place, who the main characters (protagonist and antagonist) are, and what the main character(s) is/are trying to accomplish. You should then explain what or who is in the way such as what the antagonist may be trying to accomplish, what the central conflict is, and what the climax of the play is.

Next you should make a statement about the effectiveness of a production element (scene design, acting, costumes, lighting, etc.). Use at least two examples to explain your statement about why the element was effective or ineffective. From there, make a concluding statement about how this affected the success or failure of achieving the goal of the play.

Make a statement about the effectiveness of a second production element (scene design, acting, costumes, lighting, etc.) in relation to the goal of the production. Once again give at least two examples explaining your statement about the element being effective or ineffective. Follow that by your concluding statement about how this affected the success or failure of achieving the goal of the play.

Now explain if the play was worth doing. That being said, reinforce your previously stated opinion of whether or not the play achieved its goal, followed by a concluding statement about the overall experience of the play and whether you would recommend it to other patrons or not.

> *"Whether the critic is good or bad doesn't depend on his opinions, but on the reasons he can offer for those opinions."*
> ~ Harold Clurman

> *"What is an artist trying to do? How well has he or she done it? Was it worth doing?"*
> ~ Johann Wofgang von Goerthe

FORMAT:

1. Typewritten 12 point, easily read font. Double-spaced and STAPLED in upper left corner. ******Handwritten papers will not be accepted.******

2. Your name, the date, our course and the assignment title should appear at the top of the first page.

3. The heading of the paper should be: "The Title of the Play Viewed: A Play Critique".

4. Grammar and Spell check. Your critique should be carefully written and edited. Remember that criticism involves both what you say and how you say it. Grammar and clarity of expression behind the thoughts explored will be taken into consideration in determining its grade. Be SURE you spell check and read your own writing before you hand in the final draft.

5. Ticket stub and program must be stapled to the back of the critique.

6. Discuss in paragraph form and stick to ONE topic per paragraph. Don't use the same paragraph in which you are discussing the set to also discuss lighting.

7. The length of the critique will be determined by the instructor.

8. The critique must be turned in within two weeks of seeing the play. Points will be deducted if turned in later than that. The last day to hand in critiques is the last day of class.

9. Failure to follow this format may result in a grade of 0.

INSTRUCTIONS and TIPS:

1. THE POINT: The point of this assignment is to understand how all aspects of theater contribute to the audience's experience. By writing from the perspective of an audience participant, you are also enhancing yourself as a performer. Thus, you must treat this assignment with integrity, as we treat all things associated with our beloved art form that is Theatre.

2. Do NOT just answer questions with a yes or no. Discuss means discuss. Be specific.
    Do not just say that you did or did not like something. Tell WHY you feel the way you do. Give details to reinforce your opinions. Tell HOW effects were achieved. Pretend that your reader NEVER saw the production, so you have to give extremely specific descriptions, detailing what you observed.

3. Beyond saying, "I liked when" or "I did not like" tell the reader why you felt this way. Give specific reasons and examples to support your opinion. EXAMPLE: "The large dark backdrop, shadowy lighting and somber costumes brought down the lighthearted mood of the comedy." Thoughtfully explore why's at length.

4. Spend as few words as possible in the introduction rehashing the plot of the play. Only give the briefest synopsis. The point is NOT to summarize, but analyze. (Brief plot overview example: ROMEO AND JULIET is an infamous love story that reminds us of the inescapable power of destiny. These desperate teenage lovebirds stand against a long term family feud intent on following their hearts, yet are never meant to live happily ever after.)
    Two sentences. It can be done.

5. Avoid wishy-washy phrases such as "I suppose," or "I guess" or "it sort of" or "it kind of." Such words make you sound unsure. Assert an opinion one way or the other. Strengthen your writing!

SUGGESTIONS & TIPS FOR WRITING A CRITICAL REVIEW

> *It is STRONGLY recommended that you read over this sheet shortly <u>before</u> you see the show so that what you are looking for is fresh in your mind.*

Use the following as a guide and inspiration for the body of your critique.
You do NOT have to utilize all of the ideas presented.
This is to help you zero in on the ideas you most want to bring up in your critique.

ACTING - In describing and evaluating the acting in the production, consider the following ideas:

Did you believe the actors? Under the circumstances of the play, did they respond honestly and naturally to each other or were they "acting"? Describe a moment or moments that support your opinion.

Were there memorable moments or specific instances in the play that provoked you as an audience member to respond in some way (be it a guffaw, a giggle, a tear, a sigh, a gasp, etc.)? Were these moments honest or were they manipulative? Were they organic to the situation, or obvious bits created to get a response?

How did the performer's voice, movement, and non-spoken acting help interpret the role? What subtleties contribute to the character created?

How did the actors and acting choices affect your appreciation of the play?

DIRECTING - In describing and evaluating the directing in the production, consider the following ideas:

Did the performers play together as an ensemble? Did the performers seem to be working towards the same overall artistic goal?

Were you an outsider/observer to the play, or did you feel completely drawn into the production?

Was it easy to see and hear what was going on? Describe.

Were the entrances and exits smooth?

Were the scene changes seamless, smooth and short, or were they too long and distracted from the overall production? Describe.

Was the stage space used well? Were some areas ignored or overused? Explain.

Did the pace and rhythm seem right? Did it drag or move swiftly?

SET DESIGN - In describing and evaluating the set design, consider the following ideas:

What was the designer trying to accomplish? How well did they do that? Was it worth doing?

What did the scenery look like? Was the scenery helpful to the play? To the performers? Was it a hindrance? Too distracting? Too overbearing? Too plain? Can you envision something else working better? Does it have a purpose?

Did it contribute to the mood? What mood did it evoke from you? Was it appropriate for the style of the production?

Was there a symbolic element in the scenery? In the shapes or colors? What could you infer based on the visuals about the theme or symbols of the production? What did the color scheme contribute to how you felt about the experience?

Was the design aesthetically pleasing in itself? If not, was that done with purpose?

What factor did budget play in the design? Was this an extremely well-funded but a confusing set? Was it an extraordinary set built with little funding? Was the production able to make the audience feel something regardless of the financial backing? Explore, explain.

How did the set design affect your appreciation of the play?

LIGHTING - In describing and evaluating the lighting, consider the following ideas:

Was the lighting realistic or nonrealistic?

Did it help create mood? Explain. What mood did the light and color evoke from the audience? Was there any sense of mood in the lighting pre-show? How did this set atmosphere?

Were all actors properly lit? Could you see their faces? If there were times when you couldn't see their faces, was it done with purpose? How did this affect your experience of watching?

How did the lighting use color and direction (where does it come from: below, above, behind, etc.)? What color effects were used, if any?

Were light changes made slowly or quickly? Was this right for the play?

Can you imagine changing or adding any lighting effects? Explain.

How did the lights affect your appreciation of the play?

COSTUMES - In describing and evaluating the costumes, consider the following ideas:

Were the costumes right for the play? In period and style? For the theme of the play? What theme was revealed by the stylistic and symbolic choices of the clothing?

Pick one or two costumes that particularly stood out. Describe them Explain how they were right for individual characters, in personality, station in life, occupation, etc. If you think the choices were poor, explain why AND explain your ideas for alternatives.

Was the costume design aesthetically pleasing? The colors? Why or why not?

Were there differences between costumes for major and minor characters? Explain this difference or similarity and analyze whether it worked for the overall production or not.

How did the costumes affect your appreciation of the play?

WRITTEN SCRIPT ANALYSIS

Title of the Play & Playwright:

    Indicate what Version/Edition of the play you read.

    If it is a translation, indicate who translated it.

Significance of the Title: (What does it refer to?)

Genre: (Is it a drama, comedy, tragedy, farce, melodrama, tragic-comedy, or other?)

Physical Setting: (Where is the play set? What is the Place? Time?)

Plot:

    Explain the plot, and any major subplots.

    What Required Information/Prior Context is revealed in the Exposition ?

    What does the Status Quo/Stasis (the normal life of the characters) look like?

    What is the Inciting Event (the moment where the Status Quo/Stasis quo is interrupted)?

    Describe the complications as they build towards the Climax. Does there seem to be a physical climax

            separate from an emotional climax, or are they one and the same?

    Describe the Resolution after the climax. What becomes the new Status Quo/Stasis for the characters?

Major Characters: List the Major Characters with a brief description of each.

    Indicate if Characters are a Leading or a Supporting role.

    Who is the Protagonist? What is he/she/they fighting for? How does he/she/they fight for it?

    Who/What is the Antagonist? Who/What offers the greatest resistance to the Protagonist and how?

    What do the Major Characters hope to achieve?

    Are the Characters clearly defined/fully fleshed out, or are they merely two-dimensional?

    Are the Characters realistic or symbolic?

    What are the relationships between the Major Characters?

    Is there a Character with whom you identify or have a strong reaction to?

    Why do you think the Playwright chose these particular Characters?

Playwright's Craft:

What are the Key Issues, Themes and Messages the Playwright was hoping to convey?

Does the Playwright seem to be forcing an opinion, or is he/she neutral?

How do the stage directions and descriptions help the Playwright's intent?

Regarding the Playwright's use of punctuation, spelling, or broken and overlapping lines: does it help to give the play a tempo or rhythm? To develop characters and relationships? Which ones and how? Is it Character specific? Does it help shape the entire play?

Production Style:

How important are the set(s), costumes, and lighting to the basic understanding of the play? Mention any special requirement the play requires.

Is the play meant to be presentational or representational?

Is the presentation style symbolic, realistic, naturalistic, absurd, etc?

Historical Context:

When was the play written? Is this significant in any way?

Do you think the play was written with a specific audience in mind? If so, who?

Is the play still relevant today?

Do you believe this would be a good play for SCF's theatre department to mount? Why or why not? Is it relevant to today's audiences? Would it need to be done in the original period or updated? Are there foreseeable challenges to SFC in mounting a production of this show?

What is your overall impression of the play?

ARTHUR MILLER

Born in Manhattan on October 17, 1915.

In 1947, ALL MY SONS was published and produced and won New York Drama Critics Award.

In 1949, DEATH OF A SALESMAN was published and produced, and became the first play to win the Tony Award, Drama Circle Critics Award and the Pulitzer Prize for drama.

In 1953, THE CRUCIBLE was published and produced on Broadway and received the Antoinette Perry Award for Best Play.

In 1955, A VIEW FROM THE BRIDGE (one-act version) and A MEMORY OF TWO MONDAYS were published and produced on Broadway. His possible Communist associations investigated by the New York City Youth Board.

In 1956, A VIEW FROM THE BRIDGE (two-act version) was produced in London. Miller testified before the House on un-American Activities Committee but refused to identify persons seen at meetings organized by Communists. Also that year he married Marilyn Monroe.

In 1957, Miller was found in contempt of Congress after a trial.

In 1961, he wrote the screenplay for THE MISFITS, a film with Clark Gable, Montgomery Clift and Marilyn Monroe, whom Miller divorced later that year. This was the last film for all three stars.

In 1964, AFTER THE FALL and INCIDENT AT VICHY were published and produced on Broadway.

In 1968, THE PRICE was produced on Broadway.

In 1983, he was invited by the Peoples Art Theatre, in Beijing, to direct a production of DEATH OF A SALESMAN in China.

In 1984, DEATH OF A SALESMAN was revived on Broadway starring Dustin Hoffman and Kate Reid.

In 1987, he published his autobiography TIMEBENDS: A LIFE.

In 1996, a film version of THE CRUCIBLE, starring his son-in-law, Daniel Day Lewis, opens.

In 1999, DEATH OF A SALESMAN was revived again on Broadway, intentionally timed to its 50th anniversary. The revival received the Antoinette Perry Award for Best Revival of a Play. Miller also received a special Tony Award for Lifetime Achievement.

Arthur Miller died February 10, 2005, 56 years after the Broadway debut of DEATH OF A SALESMAN.

ALL MY SONS (1947)   Arthur Miller

The original Broadway production of ALL MY SONS opened at the Coronet Theatre on January 29, 1947, and ran for 328 performances. Playwright Arthur Miller and director Elia Kazan both received Tony Awards. The cast included Ed Begley as Joe Keller, Beth Merrill as Kate Keller, Arthur Kennedy as Chris Keller and Karl Malden as George Deever.

The first Broadway revival opened at the John Golden Theatre on April 22, 1987 for 31 performances. Cast members Richard Kiley (Joe Keller) and Jamey Sheridan (Chris Keller) both received Tony nominations, while the production received a Tony Award as Best Revival of a Play.

The most recent Broadway revival opened at the Gerald Schoenfeld Theatre on October 16, 2008 for 101 performances. John Lithgow and Dianne Wiest starred as Joe and Kate Keller with Patrick Wilson as Chris Keller and Katie Holmes as Ann Deever.

A 1948 film version featured Edward G. Robinson as Joe Keller and Burt Lancaster as Chris Keller. The supporting cast included Howard Duff, Arlene Francis and Harry Morgan. In this version, Anne and George's mother has died, their father's name has been changed from Steve to Herbert, and this character actually appears in the film. At the end of the movie, Kate sends Anne and Chris off to find happiness.

A 1986 made-for-television adaptation, directed by Jack O'Brien, far more faithful to the original play than the 1948 film version.

A 2010 stage version, directed by Howard Davies and produced in London's West End, was a darker interpretation of the play.

Character	1986 Cast	2010 Cast
Joe Keller	James Whitmore	David Suchet
Kate Keller	Michael Learned	Zoë Wanamaker
Chris Keller	Aidan Quinn	Stephen Campbell Moore
Ann Deever	Joan Allen	Jemima Rooper
George Deever	Željko Ivanek	Daniel Lapaine
Dr. Jim Bayliss	Alan Scarfe	Steven Elder
Sue Bayliss	Joanna Miles	Claire Hackett
Frank Lubey	Layne Coleman	Tom Vaughan-Lawlor
Lydia Lubey	Mary Long	Olivia Darnley
Bert	Marlowe Vella	Ted Allpress

LORRAINE HANSBERRY

Born in Chicago, Illinois on May 19, 1930.

In 1937, her family moved to 6140 South Rhodes Avenue, a white neighborhood, where they faced racial discrimination including mob threats and bricks thrown through their windows.

In 1949, her father, Carl Augustus Hansberry, won the Supreme Court case, *Hansberry v. Lee,* against racially restrictive covenants.

In 1950, she left the University of Wisconsin-Madison to pursue a writing career in New York City.

In 1953, she married Jewish writer Robert Nemiroff, whom she met at an NYU racial discrimination protest. They divorced in 1964, but he remained her literary executor.

The original title for "A Raisin in the Sun" was "The Crystal Stair," a line in a Langston Hughes poem. The new title was from another Hughes poem, which asked: "What happens to a dream deferred? Does it dry up like a raisin in the sun, Or does it explode?"

Unable to find backers or rent a Broadway theatre, producer Philip Rose took the show to New Haven, Philadelphia and Chicago before opening at the Ethel Barrymore Theatre in March, 1959. The production ran for 530 performances.

"A Raisin in the Sun" was the first Broadway play produced with either an African-American woman playwright or an African-American director (Lloyd Richards).The play touched on many social taboos of the time, including integration, feminism and abortion.

Her other plays include "The Sign in Sidney Brustein's Window," which ended its Broadway run on January 12, 1965, the same night she died of cancer at age 34, and "To Be Young, Gifted and Black," adapted by her former-husband as a long-running Off-Broadway play in 1969.

Other versions of "A Raisin in the Sun" include:

A 1961 film version featuring its original Broadway cast.
A 1973 Tony-award winning musical, "Raisin", with the musical's book written by her former husband.
A 1986 off-Broadway revival and a 1989 made-for-TV movie starring Danny Glover and Esther Rolle.
A 2004 Broadway revival and a 2008 made-for-TV movie starring Sean Combs and Phylicia Rashad.
A 2014 Broadway revival with Denzel Washington/

OTHER NOTABLE AFRICAN-AMERICAN PLAYWRIGHTS

James Arthur Baldwin (1924–1987) "The Amen Corner" and "Blues for Mister Charlie"

Amiri Baraka *formerly known as Leroi Jones* (1934–2014) "Dutchman and the Slave"

William Wells Brown (1816–1884) considered to be the first published African-American playwright for his abolitionist plays "Experience" and "Escape"

Langston Hughes (1902–1967) "Don't You Want to be Free?" and "Black Nativity"

Suzan-Lori Parks (1963–) Pulitzer Prize-winner for "Topdog/Underdog"

Tyler Perry (1969–) "I Know I've Been Changed" and "Diary of a Mad Black Woman"

Ntozake Shange (1948–) Obie-Award winner "For Colored Girls Who Have Considered Suicide When the Rainbow Is Enuf"

Anna Deavere Smith (1950–) Obie and Drama Desk Award and Pulitzer Prize Nomination for "Fires in the Mirror" and Antoinette Perry, Obie and Drama Desk Awards for "Twilight: Los Angeles"

Joseph A. Walker (1935–2003) first African American writer to win Tony Award for "The River Niger"

August Wilson (1945–2005) won the Tony Award for "Fences" (1987) and two Pulitzer Prizes for "Fences" and "The Piano Lesson" (1990). Both plays were part of "The Century Cycle," a 10-play series with each play set in a different decade.

A RAISIN IN THE SUN (1961), screenplay by Lorraine Hansberry, based on her play; directed by Daniel Petrie and produced by David Suskind and Philip Rose for Columbia Pictures. Running time 127 minutes.

The Cast:

RUTH YOUNGER	Ruby Dee	GEORGE MURCHISON	Louis Gosset
TRAVIS YOUNGER	Stephen Perry	MR. LINDER	John Fielder
WALTER LEE YOUNGER	Sidney Poitier	BOBO	Joel Fluellen
BENEATHA YOUNGER	Diana Sands	WILLIAM HARRIS	Roy Glenn
LENA YOUNGER	Claudia McNeil	BARTENDER	Ray Stubbs
JOSEPH ASAGAI	Ivan Dixon	TAXI DRIVER	Rudolph Monro

Lorraine Hansberry's fine play has been turned into an equally fine screen drama. If it stays pretty much in the same room, if it seems to smack of multi-movement cinema, that is because screenplay writer, Hansberry, and its director, Daniel Petrie, have agreed that its drama mainly takes place in the hearts of its people, and they wanted to keep it as close to those vitals as they could.

As token of this recognition, they have used all the key actors who performed it on stage, and worked them in medium and close shots through most of the introspective film. This is good, because they are all fine, sensitive actors who have the intuition to convey what is going on in the hearts of its Negro characters through their hands, their feet, their lips, and mostly their eyes.

What is more - and most important - they can make Hansberry's simple, telling words carry the heartpiercing eloquence of poetry or the bloodletting slash of knives. What they say of themselves, of each other, and of their views of the society in which they live has the ring of authentic conversation and the authority of truth.

The effect is to make even clearer than was done on stage, the natures of the members of the family living in the area of Chicago's South side, which is the counterpart of New York's Harlem, and to lay bare their dreams and despairs.

Mr. Poitier, lithe and electric, emits the lightning of an angry, violent man who dreams of smashing the chains of economic enslavement with a little money into which the family has come. His man is stubborn and impatient. Money is his hotly fancied god. But his heart is good and it is revealed to be noble when the vaporousness of mere money is brought home.

Miss McNeil, on the other hand, is solid, voluminous, and serene, as his mother who tries to control him and wants to use the money she has received from insurance on her dead husband to buy the family a respectable home. She represents the wisdom of the ages, the age-long patience of her race, and she has to abdicate as the mother-monarch when she grasps the dynamic of her modern son.

As their sister and daughter, Miss Sands does a fascinating job of revealing a facile young person who seeks identity and status for herself in studying medicine and keeping company with a Nigerian student who fires her with a zeal for Africa. And Miss Dee is quietly magnificent as the any young man's hardworking wife who is realistic, tolerant, and hopeful only of a happier family life.

Least valid is the stereotyped, if not downright caricatured roll of the one white person in the drama, a deceitful segregationist. This man, played slyly by John Fielder, sounds a false and irrelevant note of anti-white agitation in what is essentially a drama of Negroes becoming adjusted among themselves. The role could have been more significant had it been played in a flat, unfeeling way.

For this, as we say, is a drama of troubled and hungry hearts confused by many indigenous factors besides the passing social snobbery of some whites. It is a wonderful, warm comprehension of a people's humor, strength, and dignity under a multitude of sad and silly burdens. It should generate love, not hate.

March 30, 1961   The New York Times   Bosley Crowther
Reprinted with permission of publisher

ATHOL FUGARD

Born in Middelburg, Eastern Cape, South Africa on June 11, 1932 to an English father and Afrikaner (European) mother. He is considered to be South Africa's leading dramatist, but is also known as a novelist, screenwriter, actor, and director.

Fugard's plays were written as social protests stemming from his universal concern for humanity. He focused on the victims of Apartheid without propagandizing his beliefs. While his plays were considered subversive by the South African government, he insisted that his works were non-political and stated that all human beings are victims in some sense.

In 1956, he wrote his first plays KLAAS AND THE DEVIL (1956) and THE CELL (1957).

In 1958, he organized a multiracial theatre and wrote and produced several plays for it, including NO-GOOD FRIDAY (1958) and NONGOGO (1959).

In 1962, after publicly supporting the Anti-Apartheid Movement, government restrictions (including surveillance by the Secret Police) forced him to publish and produce his plays outside of his native country.

In 1964, Lucille Lortel produced his first major play, THE BLOOD KNOT, in New York.
  THE BLOOD KNOT tells of two brothers who share the same black mother but have different fathers. While one brother can pass for white, the other cannot.

  THE BLOOD KNOT *later became part of a trilogy known as "The Family" with two other plays:*
  HELLO AND GOODBYE (1965) *examined ideas of a post-Aparthied world.*
  BOESMAN AND LENA (1969) *followed an evicted couple who are wandering aimlessly.*

In 1971, BOESMAN AND LENA received the Obie Award as Best Foreign Play.

In 1975, SIZWE BANZI IS DEAD/THE ISLAND (two one-acts) received the Tony Award as Best Play.
  In the first play, a man can find work only by taking on a dead man's identity. In the second play, two political prisoners share a cell on Robben Island as they rehearse for a production of ANTIGONE.

In 1981, A LESSON FROM ALOES received the New York Drama Critics' Circle Award as Best Play.
  Three people's lives are torn apart amid the atrocities of a police state.

In 1982, MASTER HAROLD AND THE BOYS was nominated for a Tony Award and won the Drama Desk Award as Best Play.

In 1988, THE ROAD TO MECCA received the Drama Critics' Circle Award as Best Foreign Play.
  An older woman may be forced to leave her residence and go to a local Old Age home.

Other notable Apartheid-era plays include
  PEOPLE ARE LIVING THERE (1968);
    Dumped by her lover on her fiftieth birthday, a landlady forces her poor lodgers to celebrate her birthday.
  STATEMENTS AFTER AN ARREST UNDER THE IMMORALITY ACT (1972);
    A mixed-race man and a white woman deal with the dangers of their illicit and illegal affair.
  MY CHILDREN! MY AFRICA! (1989)
    Two gifted teenage friends are allowed to participate in a rare interracial debate.

His post-apartheid plays, such as VALLEY SONG (1996), THE CAPTAIN'S TIGER: A MEMOIR FOR THE STAGE (1999) and his latest plays, VICTORY (2007) and COMING HOME (2009), focus more on personal than political issues.

His most recent works include THE TRAIN DRIVE (2010), THE BIRD WATCHERS (2011) and THE BLUE IRIS (2012).

Fugard and his wife maintain a home in South Africa, but currently live in San Diego, California, where he is an adjunct professor of playwriting, acting, and directing in the Department of Theatre and Dance at the University of California at San Diego.

"MASTER HAROLD"...AND THE BOYS by Athol Fugard

DANCE MARATHON
Reprinted from TIME, May 17, 1982

A boy sometimes cherishes a surrogate father more than his own. But if the boy is white and the man is black, and the locale is South Africa in 1950, a day of reckoning is inevitable. No one knows this better than Athol Fugard, who has probed the corrosive effect of apartheid on his fellow South Africans in eight of his 16 plays, ranging from *The Blood Knot* to last season's award-winning *A Lesson From Aloes.* To each of his works, he brings a tormented conscience, a touch of the poet and a scalding honesty.

After having had its potent and lacerating world premier at New Haven's Yale Repertory Theatre, his most recent play has now opened at Broadway's Lyceum Theatre. The initial scenes of *"Master Harold"...and the Boys*, are amiable, even cozy. It is a rainy late afternoon, and two blacks are tidying up the St. Georges Park Tea Room, a modest luncheonette. The elder and brighter, Sam (Zakes Mokae), putters about while Willie (Danny Glover), a simpler soul, mops the floor. The two interrupt their labors from time to time to polish up fox-trot and waltz steps for a much anticipated dance contest.

In comes Hally (Lonny Price), the teen-age son of the owners of the tearoom. He is instantly at ease, having spent more warm and happy hours since boyhood with the servants than with his parents. Sam and Hally teasingly argue about whether dancing is an art or merely entertainment. Hally scoffs that the dancers fumble around and bump into one another. No, says Sam, seraphically, "It is like being in a dream about a world without collisions...and it's beautiful because that's what we want life to be like."

The quiet interlude is broken by a ringing phone. It is Hally's mother telling him that she is bringing his crippled, alcoholic father home from his latest hospital stay. The boy remonstrates with her and, almost in tears, finally blurts out, "I'm warning you now; when the two of you start fighting again, I'm leaving home!"

What follows is an example of Fugard's psychological astuteness. For the father he cannot strike, Hally substitutes the father who cannot retaliate. He tongue lashes Sam for not doing his work, not keeping his place, not showing proper respect, and he finally spits in his face. Sam wipes away the spittle with the resignation of centuries.

It would be difficult to overpraise the one-man magnetic field that is Mokae's Sam, or the audacious emotional tightrope walking that Price does with Hally, or the unyielding, unquestioning goodness that Glover puts into Willie. A taut grace governs all under Fugard's flawless direction. The final scene will not leave the mind's lens. Willie shoots his carfare money into a juke box. Lena Horne chants the lyrics of *Little Man, You've Had A Busy Day.* The two men take each other's arms and glide across the stage in the manner of Rogers and Astaire, while the audience sits desolate in pain.

The 1986 film of *Master Harold...and the Boys* starred Matthew Broderick as Hally and South African actors Zakes Mokae as Sam and John Kani as Willie. The film was directed by Michael Lindsay-Hogg, and varies only slightly from the stage script.

THE ORIGINS OF THEATRE

1)   The Storytelling Theory
Telling stories led to the storyteller elaborating and impersonating. This led to groups telling stories while elaborating and impersonating. From there it was a short jump to theatre.

2)   The Dance Theory
Rather than verbally telling a story, a story was told physically by imitating the behavior of people and animals, perhaps even in skins or other costumes. This led to doing the above with sounds and words, and in groups. This in turn developed into theatre.

3)   The Judicial Theory
Most Greek tragedies have some element of one or two characters pleading their case; explaining why they are innocent of a crime or wrong doing. For that reason, some believe that theatre may have developed out of the judicial system of ancient Athens.

4)   The Ritual Theory
A ritual is an activity that is repeated to gain a specific and desired result. Seasonal and cyclical rituals evolved as a means of affecting events, appeasing gods, transferring information, educating the young, etc. From these rituals theatre may have developed.

5)   The "Great Man" Theory
This theory supposes that some or all of the elements of the above theories developed without developing into theatre, but one day a 'great man' synthesized the elements and made a work of art.

**A MAP OF
ANCIENT
GREECE**

CLASSICAL GREECE:
THE BEGINNINGS OF DRAMA IN THE WESTERN WORLD

By approximately 2000 B.C.E., people began organized habitation of a region of Southeastern Europe, today known as Greece. By 1200 B.C.E., a flourishing culture had developed in a number of city-states.

The Trojan War was fought between some of the Greek city-states and Troy, a city located on the Western edge of present day Turkey. The war lasted more than ten years and resulted in the ruination of the Greek economy, even though Greece won the war.

According to legend, The Trojan War was fought because **Helen**, the wife of **Menelaus** (one of the Greek kings) left her home country with **Paris**, the son of the king of Troy. Greek kings **Odysseus** and **Agamemnon**, joined Menelaus in this war to restore Greek honor. The Trojans lost the war and their city was burned to the ground twice. All the men of the city were killed and all the women and children who survived were divided up among the Greek kings and taken back to Greece as slaves.

While there is still a great deal of conjecture regarding the war, there is enough evidence to conclude that it occurred about 1200 B.C.E. The Dark Age, which resulted because of events like the Trojan War, lasted until about 800 B.C.E. At that time a written language was once again coming into use.

It is purported that during this time the poet **Homer** (c. 800 B.C.E) taught his followers the history of the Greek people by reciting through memorization the events of the past. Homer's pupils recorded these stories, creating two vitally important books in ancient literature, *The Iliad* and *The Odyssey*. Both works deal with the time of the Trojan War, and nearly all Western literature can trace their roots to them.

The Trojan War was a favorite topic for Greek dramatists. *The Oresteia*, a trilogy by **Aeschylus**, follows the story of **Agamemnon** after his return from the war. (Centuries later, Shakespeare used *The Iliad's* plot as the source for his comedy, *Troilus and Cressida*.)

Sometime between 800 B.C.E. and 534 B.C.E., **Choral Drama** began as a ritual celebration during the Spring Festival of Life, a tribute to the god of Spring, **Dionysus**. In 534 B.C.E., **Thespis**, a choral leader, became the first actor by stepping out of the chorus to deliver solo lines. This event marked the beginning of an annual playwriting competition.

By the 4th Century B.C.E., the competition spanned three days. The plays were performed in a large outdoor arena or theatre. The competition was judged by a panel of wealthy patrons and established writers. Each playwright was backed by the government and a wealthy patron. (When three plays were connected by plot and character, they were called a **trilogy**. When three tragedies and a satyr play were performed at the Festival of Dionysus, they were called a **tetralogy**.)

Alexander the Great (356-323 B.C.E.), tutored by **Aristotle**, united Greece and conquered most of the civilized world, bringing Greek culture to the Near East, the Indus Valley, Central Asia and Egypt. Athens remained the cultural center of his empire, but Alexandria (Egypt) became the center for learning.

FOUR QUALITIES THAT CHARACTERIZED GREEK THEATRE

1. Always closely associated with Greek religion

2. Only performed on special occasions

3. Always competitive

4. Always choral

TIMELINE: IMPORTANT DATES IN CLASSIC GREEK HISTORY

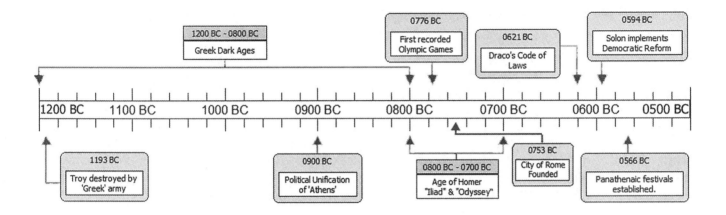

TIMELINE: IMPORTANT GREEK PLAYS AND PLAYWRIGHTS

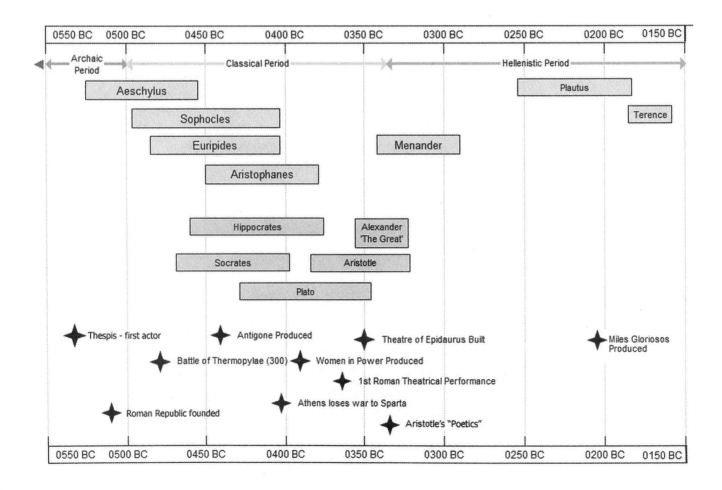

THE GREEK PHYSICAL THEATRE

Greek Theatres were carved into the side of hills, and thought to be acoustically perfect.

The oldest and most famous of these theatres was the **Theatre of Dionysus**, named in honor of the god of spring, and located on the south slope of the **Acropolis** ("hill of worship") in Athens.

*The major temple on the Acropolis at Athens was the **Parthenon**, dedicated to the goddess Athena.*

Originally, the Theatre of Dionysus sat only 500 people. Due to the popularity of the festival, the theatre was remodeled between 338 and 326 B.C.E. to seat between 14,000 and 17,000 spectators.

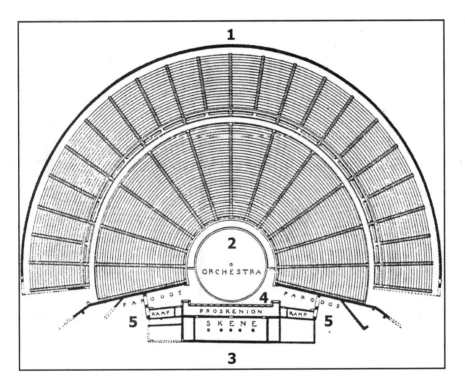

THE THEATRE AT EPIDAURUS

1) The **THEATRON** (Greek for "seeing place") was the large (350-feet wide) seating area where the audience viewed the plays. *Centuries later, the Romans would use the word AUDITORIUM (Latin for "hearing place).*

2) The **ORCHESTRA** ("dancing place") began as a rectangular area, but then evolved into a large (65-foot) semi-circular performing space for the Chorus.

3) The **SKENE** was first intended as a dressing room, evolving from a tent, to a hut, and eventually as a large (200-foot) permanent structure used for backgrounds. (The English words "scene" and "scenery" are derived from "Skene.")

4) THE **LOGEION** was a raised (4-foot) stage in front of the SKENE, where the characters performed most of their dialogue.

5) THE **PARADOS** were tall arches located on either side of the SKENE and used for entrances for the actors.

Theatre festivals lasted all day. Eating and drinking were allowed in the audience. Violence in the theatre was punishable by death.

Because of higher attendance caused by a growing population, tickets were introduced by the mid-5th century B.C.E.

Actors wore **masks** with over-exaggerated facial features.

The mouth opening acted as a megaphone and helped actors project their voices.

Masks allowed the performers to appear in several different roles and helped the audience to identify a character's age, gender, and status.

OTHER SCENIC ELEMENTS:

Machina was a crane that allowed actors to "fly". The phrase "deus ex machina" ("god in machine") now means any plot device in which something or someone suddenly appears from nowhere to solve what seems to be an insolvable problem.

Ekkyklema was a wheeled wagon used to bring dead characters into the audience's view as it was forbidden to show actual violence on stage.

Pinakes were pictures hung into the scene to show a scene's scenery.

Periaktois were triangular-shaped pieces of wood with scenery painted on each side. Revolving the periaktois allowed for rapid scene changes.

THE GREEK TRAGIC PLAYWRIGHTS

AESCHYLUS (c. 525-456 B.C.E.)

First entered the Festival of Dionysus competition in 499 B.C.E., winning at least 14 times

Each of his extant tragedies won first prize

Added the second actor to his scripts

Wrote 81 plays, of which 7 have survived:

The Persians (472 B.C.E.) celebrates the victory of the Greeks over the army of King Xerxes of Persia. This play was unique among Greek tragedies as it dealt with a recent event.

Seven Against Thebes (467 B.C.E.) follows the battle between Polynices and Eteocles (the sons of the late King Oedipus, and brothers of Antigone).

The Suppliants (463 B.C.E.) pays tribute to the democratic thoughts in Athens two years before the establishment of a democratic government. The play has an unusual structure of having the chorus serving as the play's protagonist.

The Oresteia (458 B.C.E.) is a trilogy that is considered Aeschylus's best work:

Agamemnon	The triumphant king returns from the Trojan War and is murdered by his wife Clytemnestra.
Choephori (Libation Bearers)	Orestes and Electra revenge their father's murder by killing their mother and her lover.
Eumenides	Orestes is brought to trial in Athens by the Furies, a group of underworld deities who avenged patricide and matricide.

Prometheus Bound (457 B.C.E.) is based on the myth of Prometheus, who was punished by Zeus for giving fire to mankind.

SOPHOCLES (c. 496-405 B.C.E)

First entered competition in 468 B.C.E., winning at least 24 festivals

Added the third actor and stabilized the chorus size to between 12 and 15

Credited by Aristotle with the creation of scenery-painting

Wrote 123 plays, of which 7 have survived:

The Theban Plays is a trilogy that is considered Sophocles' best work.

Oedipus the King (c. 429 B.C.E.)	Oedipus discovers his terrible past.
Oedipus at Colonus (401 B.C.E.)	The last days in the life of Oedipus.
Antigone (c. 442 B.C.E.)	Oedipus' daughter gives her brother a proper burial against the orders of her Uncle Creon.

Both **Philctetes** (409 B.C.E.) and **Ajax** (date unknown) concern major characters in the Trojan War.

The Trachiniae (date unknown) dramatizes the accidental killing of Hercules by his third wife.

Electra (date unknown) has roughly the same plot as Aeschylus's "Libation Bearers".

EURIPIDES (c. 480-406 B.C.E.)

First entered competition in 455 B.C.E., a year after the death of Aeschylus

Claimed only 5 first-place prizes, one of them posthumously

His plays were criticized for subject matter that was considered unsuitable for the stage, particularly his questioning the gods' sense of justice and suggesting that random chance ruled the world.

He was a requent target of Aristophanes. In **The Frogs**, Dionysus travels to Hades to bring back Euripides from the dead. After a poetry competition, Dionysus chooses to bring back Aeschylus instead.

Wrote 92 plays, of which 18 have survived. Considered to be his greatest plays are:

Medea (c. 431 B.C.E.) dramatizes the revenge of an Asia Minor princess betrayed by her husband, Jason, who abandoned her for a younger woman.

The Trojan Women (c. 415 B.C.E.) follows the women of Troy after their city has been destroyed, their husbands killed, and their families taken away as slaves.

Electra (c. 413 B.C.E.) presents the revenge by Orestes and Electra on their mother in a more realistic manner than Aeschylus. Orestes is haunted by his own conscience, not by the Furies.

Cyclops (date unknown) is the only complete **Satyr Play** in existence, although hundreds were written.

SATYR PLAYS lampooned serious subject matter. Each tragic author was required to submit a satyr play with each set of three tragedies, which was performed either at the end of the festival or between the second and third tragedy in a trilogy for comic relief.

Satyr plays shared the same material as tragedies—gods, heroes, and adventures—but used extreme "potty humor," foul language and gestures, excessive drinking and sexuality. These plays were usually about half the length of a tragedy and are considered a predecessor to comedy.

THE GREEK COMIC ERAS AND AUTHORS

OLD COMEDY (c. 480-375 B.C.E.) **consisted of farce, satire, and were non-realistic.**

ARISTOPHANES (c. 448-380 B.C.E.) first competed in 427 B.C.E. and lampooned important people (most notably Socrates in "The Clouds" and Euripides in "The Frogs") and politics of his day. 11 of his plays have survived:

The Clouds (423 B.C.E.) attacks the educational practices of the "new educators".

The Wasps (422 B.C.E.) attacks the judicial system under democracy.

Lysistrata (411 B.C.E.) is a sexual fantasy which centers on the Peloponnesian War (341-404 B.C.E.).

The Frogs (405 B.C.E.) is an attack on the lack of quality in literature for the theatre.

Women in Power (393 B.C.E.) questions the validity of democracy as a form of government. The characters include the NARRATOR, PRAXAGORA, 1ST/2ND/3RD WOMAN, PHIEDOLOS, BLEPYROS (Praxagora's husband), CHREMES, EPIGONES and a SWEET YOUNG THING

Old Comedy would influence such writers as Cervantes, Swift, and Voltaire, who used Old Comedy techniques to disguise their political attacks.

MIDDLE COMEDY (c. 325-290 B.C.E.) **has no extant plays from its period.**
The last writers of the Old Comedy are sometimes regarded as the first Middle Comic poets.
Middle Comedy reduced the importance of the Chorus, changed the targets from political to literary, and refrained from representing public characters onstage.
Stock characters became widely-used, including the courtesan and the bragging soldier.

NEW COMEDY (c. 325-290 B.C.E.) **was based on domestic situations and influenced the development of comedy during the Renaissance.** No complete plays survived, though several well-preserved sections of plays were discovered in the 20th century.

MENANDER (c. 342-293 B.C.E.) wrote more than 100 comedies, winning the prize at the Lenaia festival 8 times.

The Grouch (316 B.C.) was known only through various quotations until a complete manuscript was found published in 1957. Also referred to as *Dyskolos* or *The Bad Tempered Man*.

Large portions of his comedies, **The Girl from Samos, The Perikeiromene,** and **The Men at Arbitration** (dates unknown), were found in 1907. In 2003, a 9th century manuscript was found containing parts of the **The Grouch** and 200 lines of another unidentified Menander play.

New Comedy made love an important part of the plot, but made no attempts to criticize or improve Athenian society. Much of our knowledge of New Comedy comes from the Latin adaptations by Plautus and Terence.

New Comedy would influence the comic dramas of Shakespeare, Congreve and Wycherley.

ANTIGONE (443 B.C.E.) Sophocles

In 1943 the French playwright, Jean Anouilh (1910-1987), wrote a modern version of *Antigone*. This version of the story drew a subtle parallel between the play and the Nazi occupation forces in France, with Creon representing the Germans and Antigone representing France. At the end of this version, Creon recovers from his grief and goes off with his page to conduct the affairs of state.

In 1986, actor-director Don Taylor (1936-2003) filmed his accurate yet poetic version for the BBC as part of his "Theban Play" series, which also included OEDIPUS THE KING and OEDIPUS AT COLONUS.

The Cast included:

ANTIGONE	Juliet Stevenson	**TEIRESIAS**	John Gielgud
ISMENE	Gwen Taylor	**SENTRY**	Tony Selby
CREON	John Shrapnel	**HAIMON**	Michael Gwilym
EURYDICE	Rosalie Crutchley	**MESSENGER**	Bernard Hill

After the death of KING OEDIPUS and his mother-wife JOCASTA, ANTIGONE's two brothers, POLYNICES and ETEOCLES, have killed each other in the final battle of a civil war. Their uncle, CREON, decrees that Eteocles is to be given honorable burial while Polynices' body is to be left on the battlefield to rot. Antigone knows that while her brother has broken civil (man's) law, there is a higher law of the gods and of simple morality. By burying her brother's body, she expects to receive the punishment required by Creon's civil law.

The scene is traditionally set outside the royal palace of Thebes.

The first production of this translation was set inside the royal palace as though in a council chamber or senate house.

Translation and production were conceived together so Antigone's second speech reads "That's why I asked you/To meet me here" rather than the literal 'outside the palace.'

Enter Antigone and Ismene. They are both nervous and troubled. Antigone looks round to be sure they cannot be overheard before speaking.

ANTIGONE.
Ismene listen. The same blood
Flows in both our veins, doesn't it, my sister,
The blood of Oedipus. And suffering,
Which was his destiny, is our punishment too,
The sentence passed on all his children.
Physical pain, contempt, insults,
Every kind of dishonour: we've seen them all,
And endured them all, the two of us.
But there's more to come. Now, today.
Have you heard it, this new proclamation,
Which the king has made to the whole city?
Have you heard how those nearest to us
Are to be treated, with the contempt
We reserve for traitors? People we love!

ISMENE.
No one has told me anything, Antigone,
I have heard nothing, neither good nor bad
About anyone we love - not since the battle
I mean, and the terrible news
That both our brothers were dead: one day,
One battle, and fratricide twice over,
Each brother cutting down his own flesh...
But the army from Argos retreated last night,
I have heard that. Nothing else
To cheer me up, or depress me further.

ANTIGONE.
I thought you hadn't. That's why I asked you
To meet me here, where I can tell you everything
Without any risk of being overheard.

ISMENE.
What is it then? More terrible news?
Something black and frightening, I can see that.

ANTIGONE.
Well, what do you think, Ismene? Perhaps
You can guess. We have two brothers,
Both of them dead. And Creon has decreed
That a decent burial shall be given to one,
But not to the other. Eteocles, apparently,
Has already been buried, with full military honours,
And all the formalities due to the dead
Meticulously observed. So that his rest
In the underworld among the heroes is assured.
But Polynices, who died in agony
Just as certainly as his brother did,
Is not to be buried at all. The decree
Makes that quite plain. He is to be left
Lying where he fell, with no tears,
And no ceremonies of mourning, to stink
In the open: till the kites and vultures
Catch the scent, and tear him to pieces

And pick him to the bone. Left unburied
There is no rest for him in the underworld,
No more than here. What a great king
Our Creon is, eh Sister?
It's against us, you realise, and against me
In particular that he has published this decree.
And he'll soon be here himself, to make it public
To the senators, and anyone who may not have heard it.
He isn't bluffing. He means to act
To make it stick. The punishment
For anyone who disobeys the order
Is public stoning to death. So that's the news,
And you know it now. The time has come
For you too to stand up and be counted
With me: and to show whether you are worthy
Of the honour of being Oedipus' daughter.

ISMENE.
Wait a minute Antigone, don't be so headstrong!
If all this is as you say it is,
What can I do, one way or the other?

ANTIGONE.
Just say you will help me. Commit yourself.

ISMENE.
To do what? Something dangerous?

ANTIGONE.
Just to give me a hand to lift the body.
It's too heavy for me to move on my own.

ISMENE.
To bury him you mean? In spite of the decree?

ANTIGONE.
He is my brother. And like it or not
He's yours too. I won't betray him
Now that he's dead. No one will ever
Throw that in my face.

ISMENE.
You must be mad!
Creon has publicly forbidden it.

ANTIGONE.
He can't forbid me to love my brother.
He has neither the right nor the power to do that.

ISMENE.
Have you forgotten what happened to our father?
Contempt and loathing from everyone,
Even from himself, that was his reward.
And blinded too, by his own hand.
And his mother-wife, as ill matched with him
As those two words are with each other
She knotted a rope, and hanged herself.
And now our two brothers, both in one day
Caught in the same trap, claiming
Blood for blood and death for death
Each one at the expense of the other.
We are the last ones left, Sister,
And what a death is promised for us,
More terrible than any, if we break the law
By defying the king, and the power of the State.
Think for a moment Antigone, please!
We are women, that's all. Physically weaker -
And barred from any political influence.
How can we fight against the institutionalised strength
Of the male sex? They are in power,
And we have to obey them - this time
And maybe in worse situations than this.

May God forgive me, and the spirits of the dead,
I have no choice! State power
Commands, and I must do as I am told.
When you are powerless, wild gestures
And heroic refusals are reserved for madmen!

ANTIGONE.
Don't say any more. I won't ask again.
In fact, if you were to offer help now,
I would refuse it. Do as you please.
I intend to bury my brother,
And if I die in the attempt, I shall die
In the knowledge that I have acted justly.
What greater satisfaction than that,
For a loving sister to embrace a loving brother
Even in the grave: and to be condemned
For the criminal act of seeing him at peace!
Our lives are short. We have too little time
To waste it on men, and the laws they make.
The approval of the dead is everlasting,
And I shall bask in it, as I lie among them.
Do as you please. Live, by all means.
The laws you will break are not of man's making.

ISMENE.
I reverence them. But how can I defy
The unlimited power of the State? What weapons
Of mine are strong enough for that?

ANTIGONE.
Fine. That's a good excuse. I'll go
And shovel the earth on my brother's body.

ISMENE.
I'm frightened, Antigone. I'm frightened for you.

ANTIGONE.
Don't be frightened for me. Fear for yourself.

ISMENE.
For God's sake, keep it quiet. Don't tell anyone.
I'll keep our meeting secret.

ANTIGONE.
Don't you dare!
You must tell everybody, shout it in the streets.
If you keep it secret, I shall begin to hate you.

ISMENE.
There's a fire burning in you Antigone,
But it makes me go cold just to hear you!

ANTIGONE.
I'm not doing it to please you. It's for him.

ISMENE.
This obsession will destroy you! You're certain to fail!

ANTIGONE.
I shall fail when I have failed. Not before.

ISMENE.
But you know it's hopeless. Why begin
When you know you can't possibly succeed!

ANTIGONE.
Be quiet, before I begin to despise you
For talking so feebly! He will despise you
Too, and justly. You can go now. Go!
If I'm mad, you can leave me here with my madness
Which will doubtless destroy me soon enough.
Death is the worst thing that can happen,
And some deaths are more honourable than others.

ISMENE.
If you've made your mind up... Antigone, it's madness Remember, I love you... whatever happens...

Exit Antigone and Ismene in opposite directions.
Enter the Chorus of the Senators of Thebes.

CHORUS.
The life-giving sun has never shone
More brightly on the seven gates of Thebes
Than he shines this morning:
Never a more glorious dawning
Than this sunrise over Dirce's river,
When the army of the foreign invader
At first light
Made its panic-stricken flight,
And all its white shields and its bright weapons were gone.
Like a snowy eagle from the mountain crest it came
Shrieking down on our city,
The army of Argos, with a spurious treaty
To enforce Polynices' claim,
All its horsehair plumes nodding together
And a grinding of brass and a creaking of leather.

By our seven shuttered gates it waited,
Eyes glittering in dark helmets,
Swords drawn, spears couchIng.
But before the killing and burning,
The metallic taste of blood
And crashing stonework and blazing wood,
They turned and fled, the music of death
In their ears, at their backs, the dragon's breath.
Zeus had seen them, he who hates inflated
Pride, and the empty boast
Of the windbag, he heard their singing
As if the victory were theirs for the taking,
And he brought down his thunder on their glittering host,
Struck them with lightning, and sent them flying,
Scorched them, and burned them, and left them dying.

Down like a rock from the mountain crest
He came thundering to earth, the flame
Dashed from his hand,
The son of Thebes whose best hope of fame
Was to conquer his native land
And who failed in his quest.
For the war god gave us his word of command,
Like a battle chariot his terrible name
Ran them down where they stood, and they died in the dust.
Now, at each of our seven gates
A Theban defender waits
As seven champions bring their fame and armour to the fight:
And before the coming of night
Six have put their fame to the test,
Six have laid both fame and armour to rest
As a tribute at great Zeus' feet.
At the seventh gate two brothers meet
Sharing their blood in death as in birth,
Each striking together,
Each laying the other
Dead on the earth.

There will be victory celebrations today
In this city of charioteers,
And singing in the streets.
There will be ceremonies of thanksgiving, and grateful tears
For the end of fighting, as the enemy retreats
And the time comes for relaxation and play.
Now, as all voices are raised, and the drum beats

The ecstatic god himself will appear,
Bacchus the drunkard, to take power for our day
In the city he calls his own. Time to dance all night,
To shake the foundations, till the faint light
Of dawn flushes the windows, and the lamps fade.
Now Creon is king. He made
The most of his fortune, and the gods' choice,
The son of Menoeceus. As the people rejoice
The new king enters to take his throne,
The responsibility his alone.
But why has he called us here, to debate
In emergency session
His public proclamation
So vital to the State?

Creon enters, well-guarded by soldiers.

CREON.
Senators: our country, like a ship at sea,
Has survived the hurricane. The gods, who sent it,
Have navigated us into calmer waters now.
 I have chosen to summon this assembly
Because I know I can trust you. Your predecessors
Were loyal and reliable in King Laius' time,
And when King Oedipus, in his exceptional wisdom,
Restored the fortunes of this city.
When tragedy struck him, and his rule was ended,
Your loyalty to the blood royal
Was never questioned, and you supported his sons:
Till they too were brought down,
In a single day, incestuously murdered,
Each brother shedding a brother's blood.
By that same bloodright, as next of kin,
I claim the throne, and all its power
Both city and kingdom. I claim it and hold it
From today, as mine by right.
There is no certain measure of a man's quality,
The depth of his intellect and the maturity of his judgment,
Until he is put to the supreme test
By the exercise of lawful power in the State.
My own opinion is well known:
The ruler who fears the consequences
Of his actions, or who is afraid to act openly,
Or take the good advice of his senators,
Is beneath contempt. Equally contemptible
Is the man who puts the interests of his friends,
Or his relations, before his country.
There is nothing good can be said of him.
Let me make it plain, before the gods,
Whose eyes are in every council chamber,
When I see any threat to this nation,
From whatever direction, I shall make it public.
No one who is an enemy of the State
Shall ever be any friend of mine.
The State, the Fatherland, is everything
To us, the ship we all sail in.
If she sinks, we all drown,
And friendship drowns with us. That's my policy:
A policy of service to the Commonwealth.
And in pursuance of that policy,
I have issued an official State decree
Concerning the sons of Oedipus.
Eteocles, who died fighting for his country,
And with exceptional bravery, we shall bury him
With all the honours and funeral ceremonies
Customary for a man who died a hero.
The other, the outcast, the exile -

His brother Polynices, who returned here
At the head of a foreign army, to destroy
His homeland, to burn down the city
And reduce the people to a condition of slavery,
Or kill them in the streets -I have ordered
That he is to have no grave at all.
No one is to bury him, or mourn for him.
His body is to be left in the open, uncovered,
A stinking feast for the scavengers,
Dogs and crows, a sight to inspire terror.
I intend to make it quite plain
That never, under my administration,
Will people who commit crimes against the State
Reap any benefit from their actions: and at the expense
Of honest decent citizens too.
But people who serve the State, alive
Or dead, that makes no difference -
I shall honour them for their patriotism.

CHORUS.
Son of Menoeceus, you are king now.
You have delivered your verdict and sentence
Upon the man who defended the city
And the man who attacked it, unambiguously.
The full power of the law is in your hands,
And it binds the dead, as well as the living.
We are all at your disposal.

CREON.
                                        Make sure
Then, that my orders are carried out.

CHORUS.
Younger men than us should implement your policies.

CREON.
I don't mean that. Polynices' body
Is already under guard.

CHORUS.
                                        What else
Must we do? What other responsibility
Do you lay upon us?

CREON.
                                Not to intrigue
With dissidents, or subversive elements.

CHORUS.
We are not mad, Sir. We know the law,
And the penalty for breaking it.

CREON.
Which will be death. And be in no doubt
I shall enforce it. Because there are always men
Who can be bought, who will risk anything,
Even death, if the bribe is large enough.

*Enter a Soldier in a dusty uniform, struggling with the guards,
who bring him before Creon. He is very frightened.*

SOLDIER.
My Lord Creon ... Sir! If I can hardly speak
For lack of breath ... it's not 'cause I ran ...
I kept on stopping, as a matter of fact,
Half a dozen times, and I hung about
As much as I dared. I haven't thought about anything
So much for a long time. 'Listen, don't hurry,'
I said to myself, 'the chances are,
Poor sod, you'll cop it when you get there.'
But then I said to myself, you see,
'Hang about,' I said, 'or rather, don't,

Because if Creon hears this from somebody else,
You're really in trouble.' So I hurried here
As slow as I could, going round and round
In circles, in my head, as well as with my feet!
It's funny how long a mile can take you
When you're thinking what I was thinking. However
Duty called in the end, and I reckoned
It would be safer to face it out -
It may be unimportant, but I've come here,
So now I'll tell you. If I'm punished for it
The gods'll be behind it, that's for sure.
So I wouldn't have escaped it anyway.

CREON.
Talk sense man. Why are you frightened?

SOLDIER.
Well, first of all, Sir, for myself, like,
My own point of view ... I never done it,
And I didn't see who else done it neither.
So I shouldn't be punished for it, should I?

CREON.
Is there any need for all this preamble?
You take great care to dissociate yourself
From what you say: it must be bad news.

SOLDIER.
It is bad news, Sir: and I'm so scared.
I don't know how to put it for the best.

CREON.
The plainest way. And then we can have done with you.

SOLDIER.
Straight out with it then. The body's buried.
Someone or other. A handful of dust,
That's all, dry dust, but properly sprinkled,
You know, religiously - and then gone -
Whoever it was.

CREON.
                    Do you know what you're saying?
Who has dared to disobey my orders?

SOLDIER.
No way of knowing, Sir, we've no idea!
There had been no digging, no spade marks or nothing.
The ground's rock hard. No wheel tracks either,
From a chariot, or cart, or anything.
In fact, no clues of any kind at all,
Nothing to tell you who might have done it.
When the sentry taking the early turn
Discovered what had happened, and reported back,
We were all shattered, and scared stiff.
It was as though the body had disappeared -
Not buried in a proper grave, I don't mean,
But lightly covered with a layer of earth.
Almost as though some passing stranger
With a religious turn of mind, knowing
That being left unburied means everlasting
Anguish, and wandering without rest,
Had scattered a few handfuls. There was no tracks
Of animals either, not of dogs or anything,
Who might have gnawed at it, and covered it over
With their front legs, like they do a bone.
A real row started then, I can tell you.
We shouted at each other, and it could have been a fight,
There was no one there to stop us. Any one of us
Could have done it, we all suspected each other:
 But we all denied it, and there was no evidence
To prove one man guilty rather than another.

So we all dared each other to swear
To go through fire and water, to hold
Red hot pokers in our hands, and call all the gods
As witnesses that we hadn't done it,
And didn't know anyone who had,
Or would even think of it, let alone do it.
And none of any of it got us nowhere.
Then one of the fellers had his say, and he
Scared us all shitless, I can tell you.
He said - and we knew he was dead right -
There was no way out of it, we had to do it
And take our chances - this feller said
'One of us lot must tell the King,
Because we can't just hide it, can we!'
That's what he said. And we knew he was right.
So we decided we'd have to draw lots,
And, just my luck, I drew the short straw.
So here I am. And I don't like telling it
One little bit more than you like hearing it.
The bloke who brings bad news never gets a medal".

CHORUS.
My Lord Creon, this policy of yours
Has worried me from the start. My political instinct
Tells me that this may be some sort of warning
Or sign, and perhaps from the gods.

CREON.
                                        How dare you!
Shut your mouths, all of you, before I lose my temper!
And you, if you are a superannuated fool,
At least don't talk like one. Is it likely,
Remotely likely, that the gods will think twice
Over that pile of stinking meat?
By God, it's blasphemy even to suggest
That they would care a damn whether he was buried
Or not! Let alone grant him an honourable funeral
As though he were one of their principal supporters:
The man who came to burn down their temples,
Plunder their treasuries, pull down their statues
And bring destruction and contempt for their land and its laws.
Do the gods love criminals these days?
Oh no! They do not! But, gentlemen, there are men
In this city, and I have noted them,
A subversive faction, enemies of the State,
A cell of oppositionists, call them what you will,
Who reject the law, and my leadership!
They meet in secret, and nod and whisper
Their seditious talk, and they are behind this,
Any fool can see that. Their bribery
Has suborned my soldiers, and paid for
This demonstration against my authority!
Money, gentlemen, money! The virus
That infects mankind with every sickness
We have a name for, no greater scourge
Than that! Money it is that pounds
Great cities to piles of rubble, turns people
By the millions into homeless refugees,
Takes homeless citizens and corrupts them
Into doing things they would be ashamed to think of
Before the fee was mentioned, until there's no crime
That can't be bought - and in the end
Brings them into the execution chamber.
Well, whoever they are, these men
Who have sold themselves, they'll find the price
Considerably higher than they thought it was!

Creon speaks to the Soldier.

You! Come here! Get this into your head!
By Zeus, my God, whose power I revere,
I swear to you, soldier, that either you will find
The man who buried Polynices' body
In defiance of my express command
And bring him here - the actual man
Who sprinkled the earth, no other will do,
Standing here, in front of me - or you, soldier,
Will die for it. And death, I promise you,
Will be the least of your punishments.
You will be made a public example -
And interrogated by the security police,
Kept standing, beaten across the feet,
The whole repertoire of special techniques
At which we excel so much - until
You confess the full range of this conspiracy,
Who paid you, how much, and for what purpose.
The choice is yours: and perhaps that indicates
Where your own best interests lie. Crimes
Against the State and its laws, you'll find,
Are very unprofitable in the end.

SOLDIER.
Am I allowed to speak sir?

CREON.
                    No!
Why should you speak! Every word you say
Is painful to me.

SOLDIER.
                Well, it can't be earache,
Can it sir, not what I said!
It must stick in your gullet. Or further down
Maybe, a sort of pain in the conscience.

CREON.
Do you dare to answer me back: and make jokes
About my conscience?

SOLDIER.
                Me sir? No sir!
I might give you earache, I can see that.
I talk too much, always have done.
But the other pain, the heartburn, as it were,
It's the criminal causing that sir, not me.

CREON.
You're not short of a quick answer either.

SOLDIER.
Maybe not. But I didn't bury the body.
Not guilty to that sir.

CREON.
                But maybe guilty
Of selling your eyes for money, eh sentry,
Of looking the other way for cash?

SOLDIER.
I think it's a shame sir, that an intelligent man
And as well educated as you are
Should miss the point so completely.

CREON.
I'm not interested in your opinions!
If you fail to find this enemy of the State
And bring him here to me, you'll learn
That money, from whatever source,
Will certainly not save your life!

Exit Creon.

SOLDIER.
Let's hope they find him, whoever he is.
But one thing I'm sure of: they won't find me.
I never thought I'd get out of here
Alive. And when I do get out,
Nothing will bring me back again.
I've had an amazing stroke of luck,
And I won't chance my arm a second time!

Exit the Soldier.

CHORUS.
Is there anything more wonderful on earth,
Our marvelous planet,
Than the miracle of man!
With what arrogant ease
He rides the dangerous seas,
From the waves' towering summit
To the yawning trough beneath.
The earth mother herself, before time began,
The oldest of the ageless gods,
Learned to endure his driving plough,
Turning the earth and breaking the clods
Till by the sweat of his brow
She yielded up her fruitfulness.

The quick-witted birds are no match for him,
Neither victim nor predator
Among the beasts of the plain
Nor the seas' seething masses.
His cunning surpasses
Their instinct, his skiff is the greater,
His snares never fail, and his nets teem.
The wild bull of the savage mountain
And the magnificent stag who passes
Like a king through upland and glen,
The untamed horse with his matted tresses
Uncut on his neck, all submit to man,
And the yoke and the bit - and his power increases.

He has mastered the mysteries of language:
And thought, which moves faster than the wind,
He has tamed, and made rational.
Political wisdom too, all the knowledge
Of people and States, all the practical
Arts of government he has studied and refined,
Built cities to shelter his head
Against rain and danger and cold
And ordered all things in his mind.
There is no problem he cannot resolve
By the exercise of his brains or his breath,
And the only disease he cannot salve
Or cure, is death.

In action he is subtle beyond imagination,
Limitless in his skill, and these gifts
Are both enemies and friends,
As he applies them, with equal determination,
To good or to evil ends.
All men honour, and the State uplifts
That man to the heights of glory, whose powers
Uphold the constitution, and the gods, and their laws.
His city prospers. But if he shifts
His ground, and takes the wrong path,
Despising morality, and blown up with pride,
Indulges himself and his power, at my hearth
May he never warm himself, or sit at my side.

Antigone is brought in by the Guards, the Soldier is with her, a triumphant smile on his face.

CHORUS (Severally).
But wait! I can't believe my eyes!
Can this be true?
This is Antigone. I recognise
Her as clearly as I can see you.
Her father's destiny
Was suffering and pain
And on all his progeny
Misfortunes rain.
Child, did you openly disobey
The new king's order
And bury your brother?
Do you have to manhandle her this way?

SOLDIER.
We saw it! Actually burying the body,
Caught him in the act, as they say, red handed.
Only it's not a him, it's a her. Where's the king?

CHORUS.
Just returning now: when he's most needed.

Re-enter Creon.

CREON.
What's all the noise? By the look of things
I'm here not a moment too soon.

He sees Antigone and the Guards

What has happened?

SOLDIER.
Lord Creon, I reckon it's always unwise
To swear oaths and make promises,
Even to yourself. Second thoughts,
Nine times out often, will have their say
And end up by calling you a liar.
It's no time at all since I promised myself
I wouldn't be seen dead here again:
You were that angry with me the last time,
A right mouthful you gave me, more than enough
Thanks very much. But you can't beat
A real turn up for the book, can you,
There's nothing more enjoyable than a good win
When you're expecting a towsing. So here I am
Again, as the comic said, and my promises
Not worth the air they was spoken with!
This girl's your criminal. We caught her doing it,
Actually setting the grave to rights.
I brought her here, and there was no panic
This time, I can tell you, no recriminations
Or drawing lots! This job was all mine.
I caught her, and I claim the credit for it.
And now, she's all yours. Take her, and accuse her,
Stone her to death, if you like. By rights,
I'm free to go: and well shot of all of it.

CREON.
Where did you arrest her? Tell me the details.

SOLDIER.
She was burying him. What else is there to say?

CREON.
Are you out of your mind? Do you realise
The implications of what you are saying?

SOLDIER.
Sir, she was burying the body, I saw her:
The body you ordered not to be buried.
I can't speak plainer than that.

CREON.
                                   Did you
Catch her in the act? Did you see her doing it?

SOLDIER.
Well, gentlemen, it was like this.
As soon as I got back, remembering
All those threats, or promises you made me,
We brushed all the earth off the naked body,
Which was all wet and beginning to decay
By now, and we sat up on the ridge,
Well to the windward of the stink.
We all kept a sharp eye on each other,
Ready to nudge anyone who dropped off,
And tear him off a strip too. For hours
We sat there, till about midday.
The sun was smack overhead, blazing down,
And the heat was something terrible, I can tell you.
And then, it was as though a whirlwind blew up,
Definitely a twister it was, but localised, like,
And it raised up a dust storm, which swept across the plain,
Tore all the leaves off the trees, blotted out
The whole sky, and completely blinded us.
It seemed like some terrible manifestation
Of the gods, and you had to shut your eyes
To endure it at all. Then, suddenly it stopped,
And when the air cleared, we opened our eyes,
And saw this girl, standing there,
Beside the grave, and sort of wailing,
As though she were in pain, or maybe, anger:
Just like a bird who comes back to the nest
And finds the eggs smashed, or the fledgelings gone.
That's what it sounded like-She was standing there,
Looking at the naked body, and screaming,
And cursing the monsters who had done such a thing.
Us, of course. And then she crouched down,
And picked up a few handfuls of the dry dust
And scattered it on him. She carried an urn,
A small ceremonial bronze thing,
And she poured from it, three times, on the dead body -
Honey and wine and stuff in it, I suppose -
All the proper ritual for a funeral, anyway.
Soon as we saw that, we came charging down
And arrested her on the spot. She wasn't
Frightened or anything. She stood her ground.
So then we formally charged her with the crime,
This, and the one before. She admitted
She'd done them both, and we were relieved
To hear that, I can tell you. But sorry
Too, at the same time. It's very nice
To get out of trouble yourself. Not so nice
When you drop someone else up to the neck in it,
Someone you've got no quarrel with.
But still. Your own life comes first, I reckon.
You have to look after number one.

CREON.
And you. You with your head down.
What do you say to this accusation?
Do you admit it? Are you guilty, or not?

ANTIGONE.
Yes, I'm guilty. I don't pretend otherwise.

CREON.
You, soldier, get out. You're cleared of all charges
Against you, and free to go back to your unit.

The Soldier seems about to speak, thinks better of it, and goes, much relieved.

Now, tell me, a simple yes or no.
Did you hear of my order forbidding the burial?

ANTIGONE.
Of course I heard it. How could I not?

CREON.
And yet you dared to disobey the law?

ANTIGONE.
Yes, I did. Because it's your law,
Not the law of God. Natural Justice,
Which is of all times and places, numinous,
Not material, a quality of Zeus,
Not of kings, recognises no such law.
You are merely a man, mortal,
Like me, and laws that you enact
Cannot overturn ancient moralities
Or common human decency.
They speak the language of eternity,
Are not written down, and never change.
They are for today, yesterday, and all time.
No one understands where they came from,
But everyone recognises their force:
And no man's arrogance or power
Can make me disobey them. I would rather
Suffer the disapproval and punishment
Of men, than dishonour such ancient truths.
I shall die, of course, some time,
Whether you make laws or not. If my death
Comes sooner rather than later, I shall welcome it.
My life has been misery - is misery now.
I shall be more than happy to leave it.
There will be no pain, and no despair
In that. But to leave my mother's son
Out there in the open, unburied,
That would have been unendurable,
It's the judge, not the accused who's behaving foolishly.

CHORUS.
This is her father speaking. Stubborn
Like him, she won't give way, not even
With the whole power of the State against her.

CREON.
Well, we shall see. Any man can be broken,
And often the most committed and determined
Break soonest. Even iron, you know,
Left lying in the fire too long
Becomes over tempered, and will snap
As soon as a little pressure is applied.
You can break it in pieces. And the wildest horse
In the end submits to the bit and halter
Just like the rest. People without power,
Ordinary citizens, must necessarily obey
Those in authority over them.
This woman is very proud. That was obvious
In the first place when she broke the law,
And is even clearer now. She glories
In the crime she has committed, and insults me
To my face, as well as ignoring my decree.
If she is allowed to flout the law
In this way, all authority
In the State will collapse. I will not have that!
There will be no exchanging of roles here,
Me playing the woman while she plays the king!
She is my niece, my sister's child.
But I am the law. And that responsibility
Is above kinship. Were she even closer,
The closest, my own daughter, my duty

Would be plain. The law has its weapons,
And they will strike, at her,
And at her sister too - her accomplice,
I've no doubt, in this illegal act -
To the full extent of the punishment proscribed.
The other one, Ismene, bring her here.
I saw her in the corridor, talking to herself
And sobbing emotionally, like a madwoman!
Guilty consciences, you see, can never be hidden
Completely, the human face reveals
Conspiracies before they are enacted
Again and again. But there is nothing
More disgusting than the confessed criminal
Who tries to justify his actions,
As this woman has done here today.

ANTIGONE.
What more do you want? Kill me, and have done with it.

CREON.
Nothing more than your death. That'll be enough.

ANTIGONE.
Then what are you waiting for? Nothing you say
Will be of the slightest interest to me,
And my arguments you will not listen to.
I've done what I said I'd do. I've buried my brother.
I aspire to no greater honour, and if
I am to be famous, let it be for that.
All these, these senators of yours,
They all agree with me in their hearts.
But there is no gag like terror, is there
Gentlemen? And tyrants must have their way,
Both in word and action, that's their privilege!

CREON.
You are quite mistaken. None of the Thebans
Anywhere in the city, thinks as you do.

ANTIGONE.
They all do! But they keep their mouths shut.

CREON.
Not at all! And you should be ashamed
Setting yourself up against the majority,
Disregarding the will of the people!

ANTIGONE.
I love my brother. I honour him dead
As I loved him living. There's no shame in that.

CREON.
And the one he murdered? Wasn't he your brother?

ANTIGONE.
My mother bore them both, and I loved them both.

CREON.
If you honour one, you insult the other.

ANTIGONE.
Neither of those dead men would say that.

CREON.
Eteocles would. His brother was a traitor.
Does he merit no greater respect then that?

ANTIGONE.
But he was not an animal. They both died
Together. And they were both men.

CREON.
Yes, and the one died defending his country
While the other traitorously attacked it!

ANTIGONE.
The dead have their rights, and we have our duties
Towards them, dictated by common decency!

CREON.
And if good and bad are to be honoured equally,
Where are our values? Patriotism! Civic duty!

ANTIGONE.
Death is another country. Such things
May not be valued there. May even be crimes.

CREON.
An enemy is still an enemy. Dead or alive.

ANTIGONE.
No, I was born with love enough
To share: no hate for anyone.

CREON.
Very well. Share your love by all means,
Share it with the dead. I wish them well of it.
Women must learn to obey, as well as men.
They can have no special treatment. Law is law
And will remain so while I am alive -
And no woman will get the better of me.

Ismene is brought in under guard.
She has been crying, and looks gaunt and worn.

CHORUS *(Severally)*
Look Senators, Ismene, weeping for her sister!
Her face is raw with tears,
Flayed with misery!
Her loveliness is scarred now - this disaster
Darkens her fair skin with premonitions and fears
And flushes her cheeks with anguish, not beauty.

Ismene is dragged before Creon.

CREON.
And you! Snake! Slithering silently
About my house, to drink my blood
In secret! Both of you the same!
I looked the other way: and like terrorists
You laid undercover plans to destroy me.
Well, do you too confess your complicity
In this crime? Or protest your innocence?

ISMENE.
Yes, I confess. If she will allow me
To say so. I was fully involved,
And if she is guilty, so am I.

ANTIGONE.
No! That isn't justice! When I asked
For help, you refused me: and so I told you
I didn't want you, I'd do it alone.

ISMENE.
But now that you're in danger, Antigone,
I'm proud to stand beside you in the dock.

ANTIGONE.
The dead man knows who buried him. What use
Are people who are all words and no action?

ISMENE.
Please, my sister, don't despise me!
Let me share the honour and die with you.

ANTIGONE.
You've no right to claim the honour for doing
What you were afraid to do. One death
Will be enough. Why should you die?

ISMENE.
Because life without you won't be worth living.

ANTIGONE.
Ask Creon to protect you. He is your uncle.

ISMENE.
Do I deserve such contempt? Do you enjoy
Making fun of me, sneering at my misery.

ANTIGONE.
You're right. It's a reflection of my own pain,
If such bitter pleasures are all I have left.

ISMENE.
Let me help you then. It's not too late.

ANTIGONE.
Save your own life. Do that for yourself
Without any criticism from me: or envy.

ISMENE.
For God's sake, Antigone, will you not allow me
Even to share my death with my sister?

ANTIGONE.
No. I won't. You chose to live
When I chose to die: and that's the end of it.

ISMENE.
But I wasn't afraid to speak! I warned you
That this would happen. I knew how it would be!

ANTIGONE.
And most, the majority, would agree with you.
But some would be of my opinion.

ISMENE.
But we're both in the wrong, and both condemned!

ANTIGONE.
No, you must live. I have been dead
For a long time, inwardly. I am well suited
To pay honour to the dead, and die for it.

CREON.
These women are neurotic, lunatics, both of them!
One of them going off her head before
Our eyes, the other one born unbalanced.

ISMENE.
Well, are you surprised! Anyone would crack,
The most tough-minded person, under such treatment.

CREON.
You lost your senses when you allowed yourself
To be influenced by her lunacy.

ISMENE.
There's no life for me here! Not without my sister!

CREON.
Don't speak of her. She's as good as dead.

ISMENE.
Will you kill the woman your son plans to marry?

CREON.
There are other women: no lack of choice
For a young man. Other fields to plough.

ISMENE.
But they're devoted to each other. You can't
Change love as you change your clothes!

CREON.
No son of mine can marry a criminal.

ANTIGONE.
Oh Haemon, when you hear how your father insults you!

CREON.
Let him hear. What does his mistress matter to me?

CHORUS.
Lord Creon, you insult your own!
They are formally betrothed. Will you tear
The woman from your own son's arms?

CREON.
Death parts all lovers, sooner or later.

CHORUS.
If that's how the land ties, the poor child's doomed,
Her death warrant sealed and delivered.

CREON.
By you, gentlemen, if you remember,
As well as by me. You heard the order,
Agreed it with me, if only by your silence,
Did you not, before the criminal was known?
We'll have no more shilly shallying. Take them away,
Lock them up, and keep them under close guard.
It's time they understood they are women,
And their proper place in this society.
There's nothing like the immediate threat
Of death to soften up their rhetoric,
And make them look reality in the face.

Ismene and Antigone are dragged away by the Guards. Creon remains on stage during the following Chorus.

CHORUS.
They can call themselves lucky, the fortunate few
Who live their lives through
Never drinking from the bitter cup of pain.
But when one unlucky family
Incurs the gods' malignity
From generation to generation
They must swallow the bitter potion,
Again, and then again!
Just as rollers crash, and seaspray whips
On an exposed beach, and black clouds lower
And the gale from the north screams through frozen lips,
While the sea casts up from its depths a shower
Of pebbles on the shore, and black sand
From the chasms of ocean, darkens the strand.

On every descendant of the ancient line
Of Labdacus, divine
And merciless retribution falls.
In the unremembered past
Some unforgiving Olympian cast
The weight of his vengeance on the whole race,
So that agony, destruction, disgrace,
Destroys son and daughter, and darkens their halls
With tragedy. The cold hands of the dead
Reach out for the living, and no one is spared.
Another generation sheds its blood,
New fight is snuffed out, the young root bared
For the same bloody axe. The characteristic sin
Of Oedipus, arrogance, brings its bleak harvest in.

For Zeus is all powerful, no man can match him,
He never sleeps, as man must sleep,
And time, which leaves its mark
On fair complexions and dark,
Can never engrave his face, or dim
The brightness of his palace, where the gods keep
Their ageless court, at the utmost peak

Of sublime Olympus. Zeus is master there,
And well did that wise man speak
Who said that past and future time
He holds in his hand by right,
And that those who climb
In their greatness or wickedness
Beyond the permitted height
He brings to destruction and despair.

But all men hope, and some have ambition,
Far-ranging birds that never tire.
Those wings bear some men steadily onward,
But some others aimlessly swoop and glide
Down to frivolous pastures, landscapes of obsession,
Pathways to disaster, and the merciless fire.
And no man can claim to have understood
Hope or ambition, till the flames burn
Under his feet, and the once solid wood
Of his life is reduced to its last condition,
Ashes, and dust. A wise man said
From out of the depths of his inspiration,
When a man commits crimes, and is proud of the action,
A flaming sword hangs over his head:
No future but the grave, and a funeral urn.

Haemon is seen approaching.

Creon, here comes your youngest son.
Is he desperate with grief
That his future bride
Should be so brutally denied,
And all his hopes of happiness gone?
For the last of your sons, what relief
From his consuming fears
And the bitter penance of tears?
Does he come to beg for mercy
For his beloved Antigone?

CREON.
We shall know that from his own lips
Without any need of fortune-tellers.

Haemon enters and the two men face each other. Both are aware of the delicacy and magnitude of the situation.

My dear son. I don't doubt you have heard
The news of our final decision, the condemnation
Of the woman you intended to marry. You come here,
I hope, not in any spirit of anger
Against your father, but understanding
That we are always comrades, and my love for you is unshaken.

HAEMON.
I know I am your son, Father,
I understand the depth of your experience
In matters of State, and I try to follow
And benefit from it, whenever I can.
Any marriage would be worthless to me
That did not have your approval, and love.

CREON.
Good fellow. Hang on to that! A father's opinion
Should always be influential with his son:
And fathers with young sons, when they pray for them,
Ask especially that they should grow up to be
Loyal, obedient, under pressure the first
To strike at their father's enemies,
Just as they are the first to support his friends.
A father whose sons yield no such profits
From the investment of his parenthood
Breeds grief and sorrow as his offspring,
And becomes himself a figure of fun,

Especially to his enemies. Don't be taken in
Boy. Don't let any woman ensnare you
By exploiting her sexuality, or any of the attractions
That lure infatuated men into submission.
God help the lovesick fool who marries
A dominating woman. Passion never lasts,
And a cold bedroom breeds cold hearts,
Anger, and bitterness, for there's no hatred
So violent as the hatred of two people
Who were once in love. Get rid of her,
My Boy, this girl's an enemy, no good
To you, or your best interests. Spit her out like poison!
Let her find herself a husband that suits her
Among the dead. Don't deceive yourself.
She has been openly apprehended
Performing a criminal act against the State.
She is a confessed traitor, and if I
Were to spare her life, I too would betray
The State, and its law, and everything I stand for.
I will not do it. And she must die.
Let her pray to Zeus till she drops,
Let her assert she stands for family love
And ancient virtues, and all the rest of it.
If I tolerate treachery in my own house,
Under my very nose, how can I crush subversion
Anywhere else in the city, or in the State
At large? A man who rules wisely
Within his own family, is more likely
To make sensible judgments in political matters
In his direction of the State. To pervert the law,
To twist it to serve one's own ends
Or the interests of one's relations -
That cannot be allowed, neither in States,
Nor in families: and will not be allowed
By me, in any circumstances.
Unquestioning obedience to whomsoever the State
Appoints to be its ruler is the law
As far as I'm concerned, and this applies
To small things as well as great ones,
Just or unjust, right or wrong.
The man who is firm in his dealings with his family
Will be equally firm in power, his wisdom
Will be equally remarkable, whether as king,
Or indeed as subject. In times of war
And national danger, he will be the man
You can rely on, the man you would feel safe with
Fighting beside you in the front rank
When the battle becomes critical. Indiscipline,
Anarchy, disobedience, what greater scourge
Than that for humankind? States collapse
From within, cities are blown to rubble,
Efficient armies are disorganised,
And potential victory turned to disaster
And carnage, and all by disobedience,
Anarchy, indiscipline. Whereas the well-drilled regiment
That asks no questions stands firm,
Knows nothing, and needs to know nothing, and wins,
Thus saving the lives of millions of honest people.
Authority is essential in any State,
And will be upheld in this one, by me.
There will be no yielding to female fantasies,
Not by so much as an inch. And if we must be deposed,
Let it be by a man's hand, eh son?
Not by a conspiracy of women!

CHORUS.
If an old man is fit to judge, Lord Creon,
You have spoken rationally, sensibly, and with the wisdom
Gathered from long experience.

HAEMON.
Father, the most enviable of a man's gifts
Is the ability to reason clearly,
And it's not for me to say you are wrong,
Even if I were clever enough, or experienced enough,
Which I'm not. But it's also true to say
That some men think differently about these things,
And as your son, my most useful function,
It seems to me, is to keep you in touch
With what other people are thinking,
What they say, and do, and approve or disapprove of,
And sometimes what they leave unsaid.
The prospect of your disapproval is a great
Silencer of most men's tongues, and some things
Are never said, for fear of the consequences.
But I can sometimes hear what people whisper
Behind their hands: and everywhere, I hear sympathy
Expressed for this unfortunate girl,
Condemned, as she is, to a horrifying death
That no woman has ever suffered before,
And unjustly, in most people's eyes.
In burying her brother, who was killed
In action, she did something most people consider
Decent and honourable - rather than leaving him
Naked on the battlefield, for the dogs to tear at
And kites and scavengers to pick to the bone.
She should be given a medal for it,
Those same people say, and her name inscribed
On the roll of honour. Such things are whispered
In secret, Father, and they have reached my ears.
Sir, your reputation matters to me
As much as your good health and happiness do,
Indeed, your good name matters more.
What can a loving son be more jealous of
Than his father's reputation, and what could please
A father more than to see his son's concern
That people will think well of him?
Then let me beg you to have second thoughts,
And not be certain that your own opinion
Is the only right one, and that all men share it.
A man who thinks he has the monopoly
Of wisdom, that only what he says
And what he thinks is of any relevance,
Reveals his own shallowness of mind
With every word he says. The man of judgment
Knows that it is a sign of strength,
Not weakness, to value other opinions,
And to learn from them: and when he is wrong,
To admit it openly and change his mind.
You see it when a river floods, the trees
That bend, survive, those whose trunks
Are inflexible, are snapped off short
By the weight of water. And a sailor in a storm
Who refuses to reef his sail, and run
With the wind, is likely to end up capsized.
I beg you Father, think twice about this.
Don't let your anger influence you. If a man
Of my age may lay some small claim
To common sense, let me say this:
Absolute certainty is fine, if a man
Can be certain that his wisdom is absolute.

But such certainty and such wisdom
Is rare among men: and that being so,
The next best, is to learn to listen,
And to take good advice when it is offered.

CHORUS.
There's a lot of sense, my Lord Creon,
In what this young man has said: as indeed,
There was in everything that you said too.
The fact is, you are both in the right,
And there's a good deal to be said for either.

CREON.
Is there indeed? Am I expected to listen
And take lessons in political tactics
At my age, from a mere boy?

HAEMON.
I'm a man, Father, and my arguments are just.
They stand upon their merits, not my age.

CREON.
Oh, they stand upon their merits do they? What merit
Is there, please tell me, in breaking the law?

HAEMON.
If she'd done something shameful I wouldn't defend her.

CREON.
She has brought the law into contempt! That's shameful!

HAEMON.
Listen to the people in the street, Father,
The ordinary Thebans! They say she hasn't!

CREON.
I have never based my political principles
On the opinions of people in the street!

HAEMON.
Now you're the one who's speaking like a boy!

CREON.
I'm speaking like a king. It's my responsibility,
And I will act according to my own convictions!

HAEMON.
When the State becomes one man it ceases to be a State!

CREON.
The State is the statesman who rules it, it reflects
His judgment, it belongs to him!

HAEMON.
Go and rule in the desert then! There's nobody there
To argue with you! What a king you'll be there!

CREON.
This boy of mine is on the woman's side!

HAEMON.
Yes, if you are a woman, I am.
I'm on your side Father, I'm fighting for you.

CREON.
You damned impertinent devil! Every word
You say is against me. Your own father!

HAEMON.
When I know you are wrong, I have to speak.

CREON.
How am I wrong? By maintaining my position
And the authority of the State? Is that wrong?

HAEMON.
When position and authority
Ride roughshod over moral feeling...

CREON.
You're weak, and uxorious, and contemptible,
With no will of your own. You're a woman's mouthpiece!

HAEMON.
I'm not ashamed of what I'm saying.

CREON.
Every word you have said pleads for her cause.

HAEMON.
I plead for you, and for myself
And for common humanity, respect for the dead!

CREON.
You will never marry that woman, she won't
Live long enough to see that day!

HAEMON.
                                    If she dies,
She won't die alone. There'll be two deaths, not one.

CREON.
Are you threatening me? How dare you threaten...

HAEMON.
No, that's not a threat. I'm telling you
Your policy was misbegotten from the beginning.

CREON.
Misbegotten! Dear God, if anything's misbegotten
Here, it's my son. You'll regret this, I promise you.

HAEMON.
If you weren't my father, I'd say you were demented.

CREON.
Don't father me! You're a woman's plaything,
A tame lap dog!

HAEMON.
                                    Is anyone else
Allowed to speak? Must you have the last word
In everything, must all the rest of us be gagged?

CREON.
I must, and I will! And you, I promise you,
Will regret what you have spoken here
Today. I will not be sneered at or contradicted
By anyone. Sons can be punished too.
Bring her out, the bitch, let her die here and now,
In the open, with her bridegroom beside her
As a witness! You can watch the execution!

HAEMON.
That's one sight I shall never see!
Nor from this moment, Father, will you
Ever see me again. Those that wish
To stay and watch this disgusting spectacle
In company with a madman, are welcome to it!

Exit Haemon.

CHORUS.
Lord Creon, an uncontrollable fury
Has possessed your son, and swept him off like a whirlwind
A young man's anger is a terrifying thing!

CREON.
Let him go and shout his head off about moral this
And decent that, till he raves himself senseless!
The two women are sentenced. It will take more than bluster
To reprieve them, I promise you.

CHORUS.
Both of them sir?
You mean to put both of the sisters to death?

CREON.
No. You are right. I can take advice.
The one who covered the body. Not the other.

CHORUS.
And for the condemned one: what manner of death?

CREON.
Take her to some lonely place, rocky,
And unfrequented by anyone. Find a cave
And wall her up in it. Bury her alive:
But with just enough food so that no guilt
For her death will fall either upon us or the State,
She'll have plenty of time to honour the gods
Of the dead there, since they receive
So many of her prayers. They will release her.
And she will learn that worshipping the dead
Is not the business of the living.

Exit Creon. (Most scholars assume Creon remains on stage throughout the Chorus and Antigone's threnody. This production proved that Creon's next lines can be played quite as effectively as an entrance as they can as an interruption.)

CHORUS.
When the god of unbridled passion makes war
He always wins.
No force on earth can withstand
His powerful, merciless hand.
When the first flowers appear
In a young girl's cheek
The remorseless magic begins:
And then, from the deepest valley to the highest peak
His traps are set,
And no man's sins
Or virtues can keep him from the net.
The mania is universal. The gods themselves run mad.
Men lose their wits, and no one is spared.

When the madness strikes, no one is safe.
The maturest of men
Will commit follies and crimes
Undreamed of in saner times.
What else could provoke this strife
Between father and son, this family divided
And murderous anger between kin?
There is fire in a woman's eye, incited
By such consuming heat,
A man's mind can burn.
Aphrodite shares power with Zeus, her seat
Is at his right hand, her lightning
Strikes to the heart, and its power is frightening.

The doors open and Antigone enters, heavily guarded. She is dressed in a plain white gown.

CHORUS.
Yet how can we talk of justice
And the needs of the State
While we stand and watch this
Unendurable sight?
My eyes will have their way and weep,
Seeing Antigone, like a young bride
Going to her bedchamber, to marry the dead
And share their everlasting sleep.

ANTIGONE.
In all my wanderings, gentlemen, this place
Has been my home. I was born in this city:
And now I begin my last journey.
I look up at the sun in its familiar sky

And feel its warmth on my face
Only to say goodbye.
In the daytime of my life, in mid-breath,
This security policeman, death,
Arrests me, as he arrests everyone, young and old
At home, or in the street. To the cold
Waters of darkness we come, never
To return across that silent river.
No wedding for me,
No music, no guests in the room:
My wedding gift is eternity
In a stone tomb,
My dowry, for ever not-to-be,
Death my bridegroom.

CHORUS.
But your action is famous,
In every street
Mouths whisper 'Antigone'.
You go down to the dead
With the promise of glory ringing in your head
And nothing to devalue your beauty.
No sword has scarred you, plague visited:
Unmarked, untouched, you pass
From the dangerous light
Into the safety of eternal night,
Alive, alone, and free.

ANTIGONE.
Do you remember the sad story
Of Tantalus' daughter? She was a stranger
From Phrygia, unmarried, like me, in danger
Like mine. She was sentenced to die on the rock
Of Sipylus, and there was no glory
For her, only the endless shock
Of the elements, and the terrible place
Where she was imprisoned: the mountain's embrace
Like fingers of ivy tying her down,
Enclosing, entombing her, and she all alone.
While the snows blinded her, and the freezing rain
Whipped her to rags, and exposed her pain
To the naked sky.
What bitter tears she shed
As she slowly turned to stone, and the grey
Rock petrified her by inches, and she died.
Her story is mine. Today
I shall share her rocky bed.

CHORUS.
But she was a goddess
Not born for death
Like the children of men
Whose desperate mortality
Is their only certainty.
Will it soothe your pain
To share her destiny,
Or soften your distress
As alive in the earth
You draw your last breath,
To live on in legend and stone?

ANTIGONE.
This is a mockery! By everything
The city of our fathers has ever held sacred
You landowners, you elder statesmen,
You rulers of Thebes, my dying
Is no joke! Am I a figure of fun
To be treated like a child, insulted and humiliated
As I leave you for ever?

Then, forests and meadows, and our Theban river,
Glittering pathway, ceaselessly flowing
From Dirce's death till now, flat lands
Thundering beneath our chariots, you
Must be my witnesses, my only friends
And mourners, as, victimised by an unjust law, I go
To my last home
In the living tomb,
To wait, while the slow darkness descends,
Cold and starving on my stony bed
Half way between the living and the dead.

CHORUS.
No one has ever dared
To go so far before
As you have dared to go.
Now you have stumbled, and stubbed your toe
And will shortly shed your blood
On the marble staircase of the law.
You carry your father's crimes
Like a millstone on your back:
Small wonder, in such times,
If the bones bend, or break.

ANTIGONE.
Nothing more painful than that, the remembrance
Of my father's long agony, and the curse
On my suffering family from the beginning.
So much grief from the unlucky chance
Of the son finding the mother's bed, and worse
Than anything, the benighted offspring
Of that unspeakable marriage: and I,
With the others, share that terrible destiny.
Conceived in incest, no repentance
Can soften the punishment: the years
Pass, the agonies increase
And there is no pity for our tears.
No marriage for me, for certain. I shall close
That book for ever,
As I meet my father
And mother in the shades. The weddings will cease.
Marriage to the woman of Argos finished my brother
And finished me too. One death breeds another.

CHORUS.
To pay respect to the dead
Is praiseworthy, an act of love,
And religion must have its due:
But no civilised State can eschew
Authority. Laws must be obeyed,
Whether we approve or disapprove.
If you refuse to sanction
The power of the State
By indulging your obsession
You connive at your own fate.

ANTIGONE.
Spare me your sympathy,
Weep no false tears,
I know the path that I must follow,
To the sunless country of eternal sorrow,
The bleak waters of eternity,
The unimaginable years.
No grief where none is felt. I shall go alone
And in silence to my house of stone.

Enter Creon, with his Guards.

CREON.
If death could be prevented by singing arias
About it, or other self-indulgent displays
Of grief, this performance would go on for ever,
I've no doubt. But I've had enough of it.
Take her away, lock her up
In her stone vault, with half a mountain
For a roof, then brick up the door! Let her die
There, if she chooses. Or if she prefers,
Let her stay alive in her grave, why not I
Bemuse the grave's the only fit place for her,
Solitary confinement among the dead!
Whatever she does, there will be no guilt
On me, or on the State. Her death's her own.
But there's no place for her among the living.

ANTIGONE.
To my grave then. My honeymoon bed.
My prison. My crypt, under the mountain.
My home for the rest of time. I shall meet
So many of my relations there:
We shall all be guests of the sad-faced queen
Of the shadows, Persephone, in that bleak hotel
That is never short of a room. I am the lost,
The unhappiest, I think, and the youngest,
Booking in too soon. But my father will be there
To meet me at the door: my mother will smile,
And hug me close, as she always did:
And my brother. He will be glad to see me,
More than all the rest. At each fresh grave
My hands sprinkled the earth, at each
I poured the purifying water,
And made offerings. And for my beloved Polynices,
Whose broken body I set to rest,
I am rewarded with a shameful death.
There are some, I know, more thoughtful people,
Who respect my action. They must justify me.
Not for a husband, you understand,
Not even for a son would I have done this.
If the law had forbidden it, I would have bowed
My head, and let them rot. Does that
Make sense? I could have married again,
Another husband, and had more children
By him, if the first had died. Do you see?
Do you understand me? But my mother and father
Are dead. There will be no more brothers,
Never again. My love had to speak
At Polynices' grave, or nowhere.
And for that terrible crime, my dearest brother,
Creon sentences me to death,
Drags me here, and will shut me away
In a cavern under the mountain, a living death,
In silence and darkness and solitude.
I shall die unmarried, all those pleasures
Denied me, and motherhood denied
Too, no children to love me, to love:
And now, no friends. What moral law
Have I broken? What eternal truths
Have I denied? Yet now, not even a god
Can help me, and there's no man who will,
I'm sure of that. No help, and no hope.
How can there be, when common decency
Has become a crime? If the gods in heaven
Have changed their minds, and this is the way
They order things now, I shall soon know it:
And I shall have learned my lesson the hard way.

But if some others are mistaken,
Let them be punished as I have been punished,
And suffer the injustice that I suffer!

CHORUS.
She hasn't changed, even now. The anger
Inside her still blows like a hurricane.

CREON.
The sooner she's got rid of, shut up
Out of harm's way, and forgotten, the better.
Tell those guards to get a move on, or they will regret it!

ANTIGONE.
That word is my death.

CREON.
                              And now it is spoken.
Don't comfort yourself with hope. There's none.

ANTIGONE.
This is the land of my fathers: Thebes,
Built by a god. You see, senators,
My time has run out, there is no more left.
I am the last of the royal blood,
A daughter of kings. And I die his victim,
Unjustly, for upholding justice
And the humanity of humankind.

Antigone is led away by the Guards. Creon remains an stage.

CHORUS.
Others have suffered, my child, like you:
Upon Danae too
The same dreadful sentence was passed.
Far from the light of day
In a tower of brass she was shut away,
And that one single room,
Both prison and tomb
Became her wedding chamber at last.
Like you, she was a child of kings,
Yet in her womb the semen of Zeus
Descending in a golden shower
Made a mockery of the brazen tower.
Fate has its own momentum: when things
Must be, they will be. What use
Is power in the State, or wealth,
Massive armies, an unsinkable fleet?
Gods make their entrances by strength or stealth,
And no tombs or towers can keep them out.

The arrogant King Lycurgus discovered
Wisdom, when he angered
The god Dionysus with his railing.
That proud Edonian king
Was punished with madness, and long
Imprisoned in a rocky cell
To endure the private and particular hell
Of lunacy: till the healing
Silence soothed and re-ordered his brain.
He learned there the terrible power
Of the god he had challenged. Ecstasy
Is beyond man's understanding, a mystery
Deeper than reason, which overcomes pain,
And seeks truth in intoxication and terror.
Only a fool would attempt to stop
The Maenads in full flight,
Or silence their ecstatic singing. The sleep
Of reason is not darkness, but another kind of light.

And where the gloomy rocks divide the seas
In Thrace, by the Bosphorous,
The savage god Ares
Laughed to see the sons of Phineus
Blinded with a spindle. Nothing could placate
Their vengeful stepmother's hate.
Her bloody needle darkened their eyes for ever,
Blinding the children, as the gods had blinded the father.
From their mother's wedding day, their destiny
Was settled. Their wasted lives
They wept away in sightless misery.
Yet she was descended from the gods. In the echoing caves
Of the north wind she hallooed, as a child,
And on the open mountainside ran wild
With the horses.
Man's fate is determined, will not be denied.
The child Antigone pays for the parents' pride.

Enter the blind man Teiresias, accompanied by his Boy. He looks exactly as he did in "Oedipus the King." Nothing has changed, either in age or dress or manner.

TEIRESIAS.
Senators of Thebes - and your new king, Creon!
We have travelled together, my boy and I,
Sharing one pair of eyes between the two of us -
Which is the way blind men must make their journeys.

CREON.
Teiresias! What news brings an old man so far?

TEIRESIAS.
Important news, that can't wait:
And advice, which if you're wise, you'll listen to.

CREON.
I've always listened: and acted upon it
More than once!

TEIRESIAS.
And like a sensible captain
Who values his pilot, you've avoided the rocks.

CREON.
I admit it. We all do. We're in your debt.

TEIRESIAS.
Then for God's sake, listen to me now.
You're like a man balanced on a razor,
Likely to fall - or cut himself to pieces.

CREON.
Are you serious? Any man would shudder
Hearing such things from your lips
That have foretold so many horrors...
Tell me what you mean.

TEIRESIAS.
Oh yes, I intend to:
Everything my experience of forecasting the future
And understanding symbols has revealed to me,
I will make plain to you. I was sitting
In my usual seat, a place where I can hear
The singing and the secret language
Of the birds, and understand their meaning,
When I heard, quite unexpectedly,
A terrible new sound, like shrieking, or cries
Of anguish, hysterical twittering and whistling
Like the babble of a barbaric language
Only capable of expressing hatred
Or pain. By that, and the wild beating of wings,
I knew the birds were at war. Such sounds
Could mean nothing else. I could well imagine

Their bloodstained beaks and dripping claws,
And that thought disturbed me deeply. At once
I went to my altar to see what I could learn
From the sacrifice by fire. But nothing would burn.
A filthy liquid ran from the flesh
And dropped on the embers - and sizzled and bubbled
Among the ashes. Then the gall bladder burst,
Spurting stinking acid across the meat,
And all the fat melted, and was rendered down
Till the bone was left bare. I saw all this -
Or my boy saw it. He sees for me
What my eyes cannot, just as I see
Things to which other people are blind.
But in that filth I read nothing. The oracle
Was clogged with fat and decay -
And then ... it was revealed. I understood
That you, King Creon, have decreed this filth
That chokes our altars. The blood and flesh
That decays and stinks there, is the blood and flesh
Vomited from the gullets of dogs
And carrion crows, the blood of Polynices,
The flesh of that unluckiest of the sons
Of Oedipus, still unburied,
And affronting more than our sense of smell.
The gods themselves are disgusted. They reject
Our prayers and sacrifices. How could they do otherwise?
How can the birds sing of anything
But horrors, blown out with this banquet
Of human blood, clogged and stinking,
Till their very beaks drip with it?
My son, listen to me. Any man
Can make a mistake, or commit a crime.
The man who can recognise what he has done,
See that he was mistaken, or morally wrong,
Admit it, and put it right, that man
Proves that it is never too late to become
Wise, and no one will condemn him.
But if he compounds his stupidity
With stubbornness, and an obstinate refusal
To face the facts, he is nothing but a fool.
Is there anyone more stupid than the stupid man
Who cannot see his own stupidity?
Polynices is dead. Don't revenge yourself
On his remains. You can kill a man once,
And once only. Is there any glory
To be gained by defeating a poor corpse?
This is good advice my son, sincerely offered
By someone who wishes you well... Take it.

CREON.
So that's your news, is it, old man.
I am to be the target, am I,
For everyone to shoot at? Well. I am wise too:
Wise to the ways of fortune-tellers,
And the buying and selling you all go in for.
And I'm to be the latest bargain
I see, I'm to be bought and sold
Like silver from the exchequer at Sardis, or gold
From India, I'm to be part of the trade!
Let me tell you this. There is not enough gold
In the world to buy a grave for that man!
If golden eagles should carry him up
By joints and shreds to Zeus,
And spew him in gobbets on the marble floor
Of Olympus, not even that blasphemy
Would be enough to deflect me from my purpose:

Because I know that no single human act,
However much it may degrade the earth,
And the men who perpetrate or suffer it,
Can stain the purity of the ever-living gods!
But, let me tell you this, Teiresias,
A man can fall: he can fall like a stone,
Especially if he pretends to give good advice,
And wraps it up in a profound cloak
Of religiosity, when all the time
Naked self-interest, and the greed for profit
Are the only motives that matter to him!

TEIRESIAS.
Are there any wise men left? Anywhere?

CREON.
Goodness, how profound! Do you have any more
Thunderous platitudes to follow that one?

TEIRESIAS.
Mature judgment cannot be bought.
No treasure is as valuable. And good advice
Is worth more than a fortune to any man.

CREON.
And bad advice is worse than worthless,
A disease which infects the wisest of men!

TEIRESIAS.
You describe your own symptoms exactly.

CREON.
I refuse to become involved in a slanging match
Or quarrel with the recognised prophet of Thebes!

TEIRESIAS.
And yet you insult me to my face. You say
My predictions are both false and dishonest.

CREON.
That is because all fortune-tellers
Are money grubbers and charlatans.

TEIRESIAS.
Kings too have been known to be acquisitive.

CREON.
Do you realise the man you are talking to?
I am the king!

TEIRESIAS.
　　　　　　You are the king, yes.
My good advice helped to make you one.

CREON.
You've had your successes, I know that,
You've been proved right on more than one occasion:
But honesty's another matter. I've never trusted you.

TEIRESIAS.
Don't provoke me to tell you everything.
The dark waters of prophecy are better left undisturbed.

CREON.
Disturb them, I don't care! Say anything at all,
But say it honestly, not for cash!

TEIRESIAS.
Are you really foolish enough to believe
That money has ever been my motive?

CREON.
Because my integrity is not for sale!

TEIRESIAS.
Listen Creon. This is the truth!
Before many more days, before the sun has risen
- Well, shall we say a few more times -
You will have made your payment, corpse
For corpse, with a child of your own blood.
You have buried the one still living: the woman
Who moves and breathes, you have given to the grave:
And the dead man you have left, unwashed,
Unwept, and without the common courtesy
Of a decent covering of earth. So that both
Have been wronged, and the gods of the underworld,
To whom the body justly belongs,
Are denied it, and are insulted. Such matters
Are not for you to judge. You usurp
Ancient rights which even the gods
Themselves don't dare to question, powers
Which are not in the prerogative of kings.
Even now, implacable avengers
Are on their Way, the Furies, who rise up
From Hell and swoop down from Heaven,
Fix their hooks into those who commit crimes,
And will never let go. The suffering
You inflicted upon others, will be inflicted
Upon you, you will suffer, as they did.
Have I been bribed, do you think? Am I speaking
For money now? Before very long,
Yes, it will be soon, there will be screaming
And bitter tears and hysterical crying
In this house. Men, as well as women.
Other cities too, other States,
Will turn upon you for the crime you have committed.
Dogs and vultures will swarm in their streets
Dropping fragments of the unburied man
At corners, on doorsteps, in the public squares.
They will smell the pollution, and turn to you,
Its author! That's all I have to say.
You made me angry, Creon, with
Your crude accusations. So I made you my target:
And like a good marksman, all my shots
Have hit the bull. You can feel them, can't you,
You can feel the pain, like an arrow, here!
Take me home now Boy. Leave him alone
To entertain some younger ears than mine
With his ridiculous outbursts. Either that
Or let him learn maturer judgment
And how a wise man controls his tongue.

Exit Teiresias led by the Boy. The Chorus is appalled, and Creon is visibly shaken.

CHORUS.
My Lord, he's gone, promising nothing
But disasters to come ...
My hair grew grey in this city:
I was dark haired here, and now I am white,
And in all that time I have never known
Any of his prophecies to be proved wrong.

CREON.
Neither have I, man!... I know that much
As well as you ... My mind's torn apart
Like a tug of war, one way, then the other
How can I give way now? But how
Can I stand here, Me a fool, and wait
Stubbornly for whatever disaster may be coming?

CHORUS.
Lord Creon... it's time to take good advice.

CREON.
Give it then. Don't be afraid. I'll listen.

CHORUS.
Release the woman from her underground prison:
And give honourable burial to the dead man.

CREON.
Oh, so that's your advice! Total collapse,
Complete withdrawal! Do you all think that?

CHORUS.
We do sir. And do it quickly, for heaven's sake!
The gods never move faster than when punishing men
With the consequences of their own actions.

CREON.
How can I do it? It's unendurable
To deny every principle and every action
I have stood fast by. But I dare not stand
Against the iron laws of necessity.

CHORUS.
Go on sir, do it now, and do it personally,
Not by proxy - with your own hands.

CREON.
Yes... I'll go, myself, at once!
Somebody, everybody, bring spades and sledge-hammers
Out onto the mountain. I'm coming with you!
If I've changed my mind, I'll act upon it
With exactly the same determination.
I sentenced her, and I'll set her free,
Tear down the bricks with my own hands
If necessary. Perhaps it is wiser
To let the old laws stand. My fear
Tells me it is. And that's a voice
Every prudent man must listen to.

Creon rushes off in near panic with his Soldiers and his Attendants.

CHORUS.
Great god with many names,
Child of the thunder,
Whom Zeus conceived on Cadmus' daughter
Here in Thebes: Bacchus, Dionysus,
In Italy revered,
And in Demeter's mysterious Eleusis
Both praised and feared,
This is your native city, where the quiet river
Of Ismenus waters the meadows, where the fever
Of ecstasy possesses your womenfolk, your own
Thebes, where the dragon's teeth were sown.

The whole world worships you,
Wine god, intoxicator:
On the two-pronged mountain where the torches glitter
And the nymphs of Parnassus dance: by the pool
Where Castalia's suicide
Made the fountain magical, and the cool
Waters of-prophecy reside.
From the impenetrable slopes of Nysa,
Where the ivy runs wild
And the vines hang thick in your face, come home,
Theban child, Let the world sing its hymns in vain.
In the Theban streets 'Hail,' we shout, 'Bacchus, hail.'
And the city waits.

Your mother Semele died here,
Incinerated by the fire of the Universe,
Zeus in his splendour. Now in your city
Another disaster threatens, fear
Locks up our tongues, and, like a plague sore on the face,
The State's disease is made public. We have done wrong.
Now the first necessity
Is for healing. From Parnassus' rocky screes,
Or over the sighing waters of the endless seas
Come to us, healer, and heal. We have suffered too long.

All the stars of the galaxy
Whose hearts are fire, throb to your music,
And the remote voices of measureless night
Speak from the depths of their mystery.
Come, with your crazed followers, your lunatic
Women, the wild Maenads, authentic son
Of Zeus. Bring delight,
And dancing till we drop, bring rest, bring peace,
Bring healing and rebirth, let our anguish cease,
Ecstatic God, whose many names are one.

Enter the Messenger.

MESSENGER.
Senators, listen! Descendants of Cadmus
Who founded our city, and Amphion, who built it,
Good people of Thebes! No man's life
Ever moves smoothly, according to plan.
Who can make judgments, say this is praiseworthy
In human existence, and this is to be despised
When chance rules everything? One moment a man
Rides high on his fortune, and the same moment
He crashes to the depths. Luck, like the tide,
Is certain to ebb, after the flow,
And no man can tell what will happen tomorrow.
Everyone, surely, envied Creon!
He had saved his country from its enemies,
Taken power as king, and his position
In the State was unchallenged. What's more,
He ruled well, with a firm hand, and his son
Was at his side, to help and succeed him.
All that is over now. What life
Can there be, when the things that make life pleasant
Are all destroyed? A kind of death,
Moving and breathing, but not living.
That's how it is for him. Of course,
He's rich, beyond accounting, he's a king
Still, with all the pomp and circumstance
That rank implies. But what's it worth
When all the joy of life is gone?
A shadow, a mockery, a vulgar pageant.
Who can take pleasure in wealth or power
When all happiness is dead in his heart?

CHORUS.
More tragedy for this family? Tell us your news.

MESSENGER.
They're both dead. And the living must take the blame.

CHORUS.
Who killed them? Who's dead? What happened? Tell us!

MESSENGER.
The king's son, Haemon. The royal blood
Shed by a royal hand.

CHORUS.
                    His father
You mean? Or his own?

MESSENGER.
His own held the sword.
But his father's actions drove it home.

CHORUS.
The prophet warned us: and it all came true.

MESSENGER.
That's how things are. It's in your hands now.

CHORUS.
The doors are opening, look, here's Eurydice,
Poor woman, Creon's wife. Does she know,
Do you think? Has she come here by chance,
Or because she has heard rumours about her son?

Enter Eurydice with her Women..

EURYDICE.
Gentlemen ... good friends. My ears caught
Of what you were saying, a few words
As I opened the door. I was on my way
To offer prayers to Pallas Athene:
We had just drawn back the bolt, when I heard
A few scraps of your conversation: enough
To make me fear what all mothers fear-
An accident, or some disaster to those we love.
I almost fainted. My ladies-in-waiting
Caught me in their arms. Please, speak it out
Plainly, whatever it is. I can bear it.
We are bred to stoicism in this family.

MESSENGER.
Dear Queen, whom we all respect... I was there,
I saw it all, and I'll tell you
Exactly what happened. There's no point
In trying to soften the blow now
Only to be proved a liar later.
It's best to tell the truth. I went
With the king, your husband, to the edge of the battlefield,
Where we saw the body of Polynices
Still lying where he fell, and in a terrible state:
The dogs had been at him. So we prayed -
First to Hecate, who haunts crossroads
And tombs, and the scenes of crimes committed
But not atoned for, and then to Pluto,
King of the Dead. We asked them to have pity
On him, and on us, and not to be angry.
Then we washed him, or what was left of him,
With holy water, cut fresh branches
To make a pyre, and burned the remains.
Then we shovelled a mound of his own Theban earth
Over the ashes, and when we had finished
We hurried off as fast as we could
To the prison cell furnished with stones
That served as a bridal suite for the girl
Married to death. But before we arrived,
One of the soldiers, with the unenviable job
Of guarding that god-forsaken place
Came running back to tell the king
That he'd heard a terrible noise, like screaming,
From inside the mountain. And as Creon got nearer
He heard it too - faint, but audible,
A kind of weird sobbing, or moaning,
Low and unearthly, as though grief were speaking
Its own naked language. The king groaned
Aloud, and we all heard him say
'Oh, God, this is what I was afraid of.
Am I a prophet too? This path
Up to the tomb, these last few steps,
Are the most agonising journey I shall ever make.

I can hear my son's voice in there!
You, quickly, Guards, anybody,
Get inside, squeeze between the rocks.
Where somebody has already forced an entrance,
Get into the main chamber of the cave
And tell me if it is my son's voice
I recognised, or whether the gods
Are playing some brutal game with me!'
So, we went in and looked, as the half-crazed king
Had told us to. And in the darkest corner
We saw her, strung up by the neck, hanging
From an improvised rope of twisted linen
Strips, torn from her own dress. Haemon
Was right beside her, cuddling her body
As it dangled there, sobbing broken-heartedly
At his wife's death, and the marriage bad luck
And his father's cruelty had made certain
Would never take place. When Creon saw them,
He staggered into the cave, groaning
Like an animal, and sobbed aloud, 'My Boy,
My poor Boy, what have you done?' And then,
'Have you gone mad, coming here? There's nothing
Here for you but death and annihilation
And despair. Come away from there, my Son
Come out, for God's sake, I'm begging you,
Come away!' But the boy just looked at him,
And his eyes were terrifying, with an anger
Like I've never seen before. Without a word
He spat in his father's face, and drew
His sword, and lunged straight for the old man,
But Creon was quick, and skipped out of distance.
And the poor lad, hysterical with grief
And self-disgust, held his sword at arm's length
And plunged it between his own ribs.
And then, still conscious, he lifted the girl
Down into the crook of his arm
And cradled her there, in his own blood.
His breathing got harder and shorter, as his life
Flooded away before our eyes, like a fountain,
Soaking her body - so that her white cheeks
Flushed red again with the bloodstains.

Eurydice turns and walks out, without hurry. Her Women look round, uncertain, then follow her. Some of the Chorus see the exit, and are disturbed. The Messenger does not see it, and continues telling his story to the rest of the Chorus.

So now they're together, two corpses,
Joined in death. He got his marriage,
Poor lad, but it was solemnised in the grave
Where there are no celebrations.
They look like honeymooners, quietly sleeping
Side by side in one bed: evidence
Of the havoc man can bring upon man
By his own pig-headedness and arrogance.

CHORUS.
That's strange ... What do you make of it? ... His wife
Has gone without a word: giving no indication
Of her own feelings, one way or the other...

MESSENGER.
It scares me a bit... but I'm quite sure
She has good reason. A public demonstration
Of grief would be unlike her. She'll suffer
Like any other mother, for her son's death,
But in private, with her women. She'd never
Do anything foolish or indiscreet,
I'm sure of that. She's far too sensible.

CHORUS.
I don't know. Her silence was unnerving,
Dangerously unlike what one would expect.
That sort of silence is sometimes more threatening
Than screaming and tears.

MESSENGER.
I'll go in after her:
Just to make sure that grief doesn't tempt her
To anything silly, or excessive. You're right,
The silence was unnerving. She seemed to feel nothing:
And in my experience, that can be dangerous.

The Messenger goes in after the Queen. As he does so, the doors open, and servants enter carrying the dead body of Haemon on a bier, closely followed by the distraught Creon. (It is perfectly feasible, though not always practicable, for Creon to enter carrying his dead son - in which cue this line should be tendered: 'He carries a silent witness with him.)

CHORUS.
Look there! The King is coming:
But not alone.
A silent witness comes before him,
Dead as stone,
Unspeaking evidence that the crime
Like the grief, is all his own.
He suffers now for his wrongdoing.

CREON.
Pain...
There was hatred inside me, the urge to destroy
Drove me like a maniac, an insane
Plunge towards death - your death my Boy.
See here, the killer and his victim!
See here, the father and his son!
I was responsible. My actions killed him.
There is no blame for him, none.
Blasted in the morning of your life,
My hope, my joy,
My hand powered the knife,
My arrogance determined your fate.

CHORUS.
You see the truth now, but you see it too late.

CREON.
Suffering
Is the only schoolteacher.
The gods have broken my back,
Whipped me like a beast up this stony track
And destroyed my self-respect.
All pleasure, all rejoicing
They have turned to anguish and weeping.
Man is a naked mortal creature:
Affliction is all he can expect.

Re-enter the Messenger.

MESSENGER.
My Lord, you have suffered enough. But more
Suffering is marked to your name.
One agony lies here in the open,
Another is waiting, the same
Anguish redoubled, behind the door.

CREON.
There can be nothing worse. My heart is broken.

MESSENGER.
Your wife is dead, the mother of this slaughtered son.
Her wound is fresh, but the breath of life is gone.

CREON.
Hades
Is deep, bottomless the abyss of the dead.
Will you kill me too, or bring me to my knees
To suffer longer: beating my head
Insensible with pain? What can you say,
Messenger of death with the sad face
More than you've said already? My way
Is towards the darkness, my case
Can be no worse than it is. Can you kill me again?
I am dead already. Is there more blood,
More savagery, more hacking of flesh, more pain,
First the son, then the mother? No end to this grief?

CHORUS.
There's no hiding it now. See for yourself.

The doors open to reveal Eurydice dead.

CREON.
Unending
Unendurable pain.
This is the second time I am forced to see
What no man's eyes should ever see,
Even once. Is this how it ends?
Or will there be more torture, more suffering?
A few moments ago my trembling
Arms embraced a dead son.
Now death has snatched the mother from my hands.

MESSENGER.
It was there by the household shrine she collapsed,
Still holding the razor-sharp knife. And as darkness
Drew down its slow blinds, and her eyes closed,
She spoke of Megareus who died in the fullness
Of his youth, her elder boy. By his empty bed
She wept, and for the son whose life ended
Today, and with her last, dying breath,
Cursed you as his murderer, who drove him to this death.

CREON.
I'm shaking! I shall go mad with this terror!
There must be a sword, somewhere,
A sharp, two-edged knife
To cut away my life.
Living is misery for me now, for ever.
When I look, I see blood everywhere.

MESSENGER.
It's no more than the truth I've told.
Her last word
Was to blame you for both deaths, mother and son.

CREON.
How did she die? Did she do it alone?

MESSENGER.
She heard them weeping for Haemon, cried aloud,
And skewered herself under the heart with a sword.

CREON.
She spoke the truth. All the guilt is mine!
I am the murderer. Make that plain.
Somebody, anybody, take me away:
I disgrace the decent light of day.
I am nothing now. I have become nothing.
Nothing can happen to a man who is nothing.

CHORUS.
How can we judge for the best
In times like these?
Prompt action is safest.
What more is there to lose?

CREON.
Where are you, my friend? Come you shadowy
Messenger who runs faster than the wind,
Wrap me in darkness, as a friend should!
Why waste another day? What good
Is daylight to me? Why should my misery
Darken the face of another dawn? Pull down the blind.

CHORUS.
Tomorrow is a mystery. No man can say
What time will make plain. We live day by day.
The future is in greater hands than ours.

CREON.
I am nothing. I want nothing. My last, simplest prayers.

CHORUS.
No time for prayers now. Too late to pray.
What must come, will come, tomorrow, or today.

CREON.
I am nothing. Take me then. The man
Who killed, without knowing it, his wife and son.
Where shall I go then? Left, or right?
All wrong turnings now. Into the night,
Darkness, hide me. There's blood on my hands. My head
Is split, my back is broken. I should be dead.

Exit Creon.

CHORUS.
The key to human happiness
Is to nurture wisdom in your heart,
For man to attend to man's business
And let the gods play their part:
Above all, to stand in awe
Of the eternal, unalterable law.
The proud man may pretend
In his arrogance to despise
Everything but himself. In the end
The gods will bring him to grief.
Today it has happened here. With our own eyes
We have seen an old man, through suffering, become wise.

Exit the Chorus.

TIMELINE: IMPORTANT DATES IN CLASSIC ROMAN HISTORY

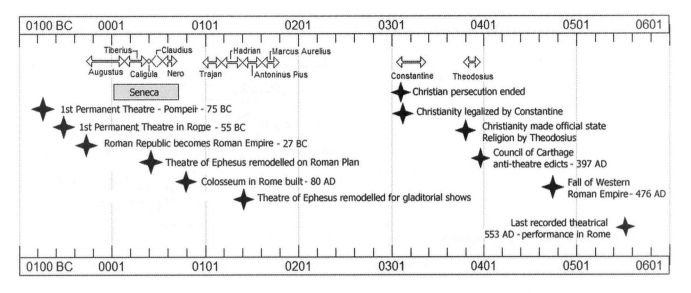

According to legend, Rome was founded in 753 B.C.E. by twin brothers Romulus and Remus.

By 509 B.C.E., Rome had become a powerful **Republic** with elected officials representing the people.

Prior to the First Punic War (264 B.C.E - 241 B.C.E.), Roman Theatre consisted of variety entertainments featuring skits, music, dance, acrobats, jugglers, trained animals, and athletic events.

By 240 B.C.E., Rome had conquered territories where Greek Theatre flourished and they became acquainted with the Greek arts.

By 146 B.C.E., Rome had conquered the entire Hellenistic (Greek-influenced) world.

Most Roman theatre was associated with **religious festivals** honoring the Roman gods.

As more gods were created, more festivals were added.

In 240 B.C.E., there was one religious festival day.

By 150 B.C.E., there were about 25.

By 354 C.E. almost half the year were festival days: 100 for theatre and 75 for chariots and gladiators.

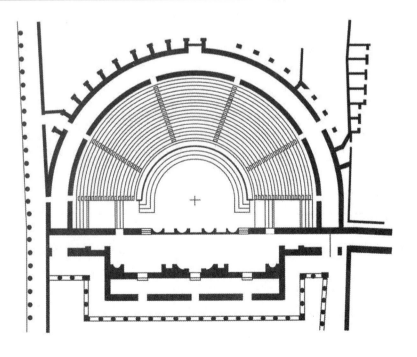

THE THEATRE OF POMPEY

In 61 B.C.E. construction began on **THE THEATRE OF POMPEY**, which was dedicated in 55 B.C.E., before the structure was completed.

The theatre was financed by **Gnaeus Pompeius Magnus** (known as "Pompey the Great") during his 2nd consulship of Rome and dedicated to his personal deity, **Venus Victrix** ("Venus the Victorious")

This was one of the first permanent (non-wooden) theatres in Rome and for centuries it was considered the largest theatre in the world.

ROMAN THEATRE AND PLAYWRIGHTS

Under the Roman Republic, drama prospered with two forms:
  Tragedy told tales of such Roman virtues as honor and loyalty, usually with unhappy endings.
  Comedy told lighthearted stories that always ended happily.

Neither Roman comedy nor tragedy contained major philosophical concerns or questioned values as the Greeks had done.

There are no extant tragedies from the Republic, but 27 comedies did survive.

NOTABLE PLAYWRIGHTS DURING THE REPUBLIC INCLUDE:

PLAUTUS [Titus Maccius Plautus] (c. 254–184 B.C.E.)
  Believed to have worked as a stage-carpenter before his acting talent was eventually discovered.
  He dapted his plays from Greek comedies for a Roman audience.
  Of his 50-100 plays only 20 have survived. Among the best known:

  The Menaechmi involves twin brothers and mistaken identity. This play was the major source for Shakespeare's *The Comedy of Errors*, which was adapted into the Rodgers and Hart musical *The Boys from Syracuse.*

  Miles Gloriosus (The Braggart Soldier) boasts of his military greatness while other characters plot against him. The characters include PYRGOPOLYNICES (the braggart soldier), PALAESTRIO (the soldier's slave), PHILOCOMASIUM (the soldier's young female captive), PLEUSICLES (a young man in love with the young woman), ACROTELEUTIUM (a coutesan pretending to be the soldier's wife), PERIPLECHOMENOS (an old man), ARTOTROGUS (a parasite or "bread muncher"), CARIO, MELPHIDIPPA and a MESSENGER. The comedies of Plautus were major sources for Stephen Sondheim's musical, *A Funny Thing Happened on the Way to the Forum*, which featured a character named Miles Gloriosus.

TERENCE [Publius Terentius Afer] (ca. 195-159 B.C.)
  Thought to be an African brought to Rome as a slave by a Senator.
  By different accounts, he was either freed eventually or was able to purchase his freedom.
  All six of his plays, based on Greek comedies, have survived. They include:
  Adelphoe (The Brothers), **Andria** (The Girl from Andros), **Eunuchus,**
  Heauton Timorumenos (The Self-Tormentor), **Hecyra** (The Mother-in-Law) and **Phormio**

Other notable playwrights during the Republic:

LUCIUS LIVIUS ANDRONICUS (c. 240-204 B.C.E.) was a Greek slave who wrote at least two comedies, translated many Greek works into Latin, and wrote the first Roman tragedies, including tales of *Achilles, Aiax* and *Andromeda*.   Both Cicero and Horace referred to Livius as the "father of Latin literature."

TIMELINE: Variety Acts and Drama During the Roman Republic & Empire

◄◄◄ Variety Acts			Drama			Variety Acts ►►►
			240			
0550 BC	0450 BC	0350 BC	0250 BC	0150 BC	0050 BC	0051 0151
← 753 Rome Founded 509		Roman Repulic			27	Roman Empire ►►►

A MAP OF ANCIENT ROME AND GREECE

GNAEUS NAEVIUS (c. 270-201 B.C.E.) was the first native-born Roman writer who wrote at least 6 tragedies, more than 30 comedies, and created the Roman "historical play," including the childhood tales of *Romulus and Remus*. His plays criticized Roman politics, resulting in his imprisonment and eventual banishment.

The Roman Empire began in 27 B.C.E., when the Senate named Octavian (the grand-nephew of Julius Caesar) as Roman Emperor Augustus. During the Empire, traditional drama would be largely abandoned in favor of new entertainments which offered violence and bloodshed: chariot racing, gladiator contests, wild animal fights, and mock cavalry and naval battles.

There are no extant comedies from the Empire, but 9 tragedies by Seneca survived.

SENECA [Lucius Annaeus Seneca], the younger (ca. 4 B.C.E.-65 C.E.)
Probably born in Spain and educated in Rome
In 38 C.E., quarreled with Emperor Caligula, but Seneca's life was spared because of his poor health.
In 41 C.E., banished to Corsica by Emperor Claudius on a charge of adultery.
In 49 C.E., recalled to Rome to tutor a young Nero, who became Emperor in 54 C.E.
In 65 C.E., ordered to kill himself when suspected of plotting to kill Emperor Nero.

Nine of his tragedies survive including **Medea, The Trojan Women, The Madness of Hercules, Hercules on Oeta, Agamemnon, Oedipus, Phaedra, Thyestes** and **The Phoenician Women.**

During the Medieval and Renaissance eras, Seneca's plays were widely read and strongly influenced tragic writers of that time, particularly Thomas Kyd's *The Spanish Tragedy* and William Shakespeare's *Hamlet*, with both plays sharing a theme of revenge, appearance of ghosts, and a bloody climax.

Although Roman Theatre never achieved the status of Greek Theatre, the Romans did make several contributions to world drama:

The chorus was eliminated.

Plays were no longer separated into episodes, but into acts.

Musical accompaniment was added to the dialogue.

All action took place in streets, even when certain scenes should have logically taken place indoors.

Eavesdropping became common (overheard conversations caused plot complications)

THE MEDIEVAL PERIOD

The fall of the Western Roman Empire in 476 C.E. marked the beginning of the Middle Ages. During the Early Middle Ages ("The Dark Ages"), industry, commerce and education all but disappeared. There was a great deal of political turmoil with no reliable political structure other than the Christian Church. The first political structure to develop was **feudalism,** in which the manor (large estate), headed by a nobleman, had absolute authority over the **serfs** (peasants) who worked the land. Lords of the manor were **vassals**, subjects of the king, who offered protection to the lords and their lands.

Little is known about theatre between the fall of Rome and 1000 C.E., but there are a few extant references to actors, minstrels, jugglers and dancers in nomadic tribes, as well as performers at pagan festivals and rites. Most of these references are in the form of church edicts against *mimi, histriones, ioculatores,* terms for secular performers. The Church only supported artworks with religious themes.

Theatre, which developed as part of ancient religious ceremonies, was abolished by the Christian Church as sacrilegious. Theatre was then resurrected as a Church ceremony in the 10th century. It is speculated that the Church, in direct competition with popular pagan rites and rituals, enticed the populace by adding **tropes** (dramatic scenes). The first recorded trope was *Quem Quaeritis* ca. 925 C.E., as "The Three Marys" (Jesus's mother, Lazarus's sister, and the Magdalene) come to the tomb of Jesus. An angel asks whom they seek. The *entire* text of *Quem Quaeritis* reads:

> "Whom seek you in tomb, O Christians?"
> "Jesus of Nazareth, the crucified, O heavenly beings."
> "He is not here, He is risen as foretold:
> Go and announce that He is risen from the tomb."

Other stories dealing with Christ would soon follow. **MEDIEVAL DRAMA** existed between the 10th and 15th centuries with little extant evidence. By the end of the 15th century, two different types of drama developed:

<u>**LITURGICAL DRAMA**</u> was sung or chanted in Latin during church services:

    MYSTERY PLAYS such as *Second Shepherd's Play*, dealt with events in the life of Christ or stories from the Old Testament.

    MIRACLE PLAYS dealt with the lives of the Saints, both historical and legendary.

    MORALITY PLAYS were allegories such as *Everyman* that dealt with the common man's struggle for salvation. These plays praised the "seven virtues" (prudence, justice, temperance, fortitude, faith, hope and charity) and condemned the "seven deadly sins" (pride, lust, anger, covetousness, gluttony, envy and sloth).

<u>**SECULAR PLAYS**</u> **OR** <u>**FOLK PLAYS**</u> were short, farcical tales dealing with heroes like Robin Hood. They were made possible when Morality Plays moved from Biblical to human characters.

In 1501, six plays by **Hrotsvitha** of Gandersheim (c.935 -c.1002), a Benedictine nun, were found and published, the only extant secular plays of the Medieval period. It is unknown if these plays were produced during her lifetime, but she became the first known female dramatist, the first western playwright in the post-Classical era, and the first playwright with a feminist perspective.

Contemporary examples of Medieval Drama are *The Oberammergau Passion Play* (1634-present), presented every 10 years in maintaining a promise made by the people of the town when they were spared the plague during the Thirty Years War (1618-1648), and such musicals as *Jesus Christ Superstar* and *Joseph and the Amazing Technicolor Dreamcoat* by Andrew Lloyd-Webber and Tim Rice and *Godspell* by Stephen Schwartz and John-Michael Tebelak.

IN GERMANY:

Circa 1440, **Johannes Gutenberg** (c. 1398–1468) invented the mechanical printing press, which helped to spread immediately the Renaissance and eventually the Protestant Reformation.

In 1517, **Martin Luther** (1483-1546) posted the **Ninety-Five Theses** on the Castle Church in Wittenberg, sparking the Protestant Reformation. Luther would later publish his German translation of the New Testament in 1522 and the Old Testament in 1534.

IN ENGLAND:

In 1534, **Henry VIII** (1491-1547) separated from the Catholic Church with The Act of Supremacy, declaring that the King was "the only Supreme Head on Earth of the Church of England". Henry used theatre as a propaganda tool to discredit the Pope.

THE RENAISSANCE

IN ITALY:

By the 14th century, artists were beginning to break with Medieval style painting and culture.
The Renaissance ("rebirth") began in the late 14th century in Florence, Italy. By the 17th century, it had extended throughout the rest of Europe.

Many of the greatest artists of this period were natives of Florence.
   Writers: **Dante** (1265–1321) and **Petrarch** (1304–1374)
   Artists: **Leonardo Da Vinci** (1452-1519) and **Michaelangelo Buonarroti** (1475-1564)

The only notable Italian Renaissance play is ***La Mandragola*** ("The Mandrake"), a cuckold comedy about a young wife and her old husband, written by **Niccolo Machiavelli** (1469-1527).

THE COMMEDIA DELL'ARTE ("comedy of the profession"), began in Italy in the 15th century and remained popular through the 18th century. A troupe of actors portrayed stock characters with distinctive costumes and characteristics, and improvised dialogue from a structured plot. Scenarios were passed from one troupe to another, and more than 800 scenarios have been preserved. **Some of these characters include:**

PANTALONE was a wealthy merchant who was troubled with his wife, children or servants. He was almost always serious and the humor of the character came from his anger.

DOTTORE was a Doctor, a Lawyer, or a University Professor, often the object of ridicule and scorn. Through this character, the comedia companies made fun of organized education.

EL CAPITANO was a descendant of the Braggart Warrior, overdressed and boastful.

ZANI were the foolish servants; **HARLEQUIN** was the most popular servant and constantly in trouble. His mischief was the basis for his humor. The character was often paddled with a "slap stick", which in modern use indicates broad physical comedy.

INAMORATI were realistic young lovers, and did not wear the partial face masks.

Lazzi was extended comic business, which often identified an actor, or even a company.

The Commedia dell'Arte introduced the professional actor into Europe.

INTERMEZZI were first intended to be performed between the acts of a play for special occasions in Italian courts, but became more popular than the plays themselves. Intermezzi evolved into spectacular theatrical events with elaborate scenery and costumes, and were the precursor to opera. (The English word "intermission" derives from Intermezzi.)

RULERS OF BRITAIN   1066-1603

Monarchs were succeeded by their eldest son, unless otherwise noted.

NORMAN

William I	1066 -1087	"The Conqueror"; Duke of Normandy wins crown at The Battle of Hastings
William II	1087 - 1100	"Rufus" (for either his red hair or his foul temper)
Henry I	1100 - 1135	"Beauclerc"(fine student)
Stephen	1135 - 1154	"of Boulogne"; Grandson of William I, he seized the throne from Henry's daughter, Matilda, the rightful heir

PLANTAGENET

Henry II	1154 - 1189	Son of Matilda and Geoffrey, Count of Anjou; Modern plays written about his reign include "MURDER IN THE CATHEDRAL" by T. S. Eliot and "THE LION IN WINTER" by William Goldman
Richard I	1189 - 1199	"The Lionhearted" (Coeur-de-lion); warrior in "The Crusades"
* John	1199 - 1216	"Lackland"--youngest son of Henry II and Eleanor, signs Magna Carta 1215
Henry III	1216 - 1272	Defeated and captured in the Baron's War of 1264
Edward I	1272 - 1307	"Longshanks"; Convened the Model Parliament in 1295
Edward II	1307 - 1327	First heir to be called "Prince of Wales"; Forced to abdicate by Parliament; Subject of play by Christopher Marlowe
Edward III	1327 - 1377	Began The Hundred Years War with France
* Richard II	1377 - 1399	Grandson of Edward III, deposed by Henry IV

LANCASTER

* Henry IV	1399 - 1413	"Bolingbroke"; Grandson of Edward III, son of Duke of Lancaster
* Henry V	1413 - 1422	Brought England to first rank European power
* Henry VI	1422 - 1461	Deposed by Edward IV; War of the Roses began
	1470 - 1471	(Restored to power briefly 1470-1471)

YORK

Edward IV	1461-1483	Great-great-grandson of Edward III, son of Duke of York
	1471-1483	(Removed from throne in 1470; wins throne again in 1471)
Edward V	1483	Probably murdered by Richard of Gloucester (Richard III)
* Richard III	1483 - 1485	"Crookback"; Brother of Edward IV; Defeated on Bosworth Field

TUDOR

Henry VII	1485 - 1509	Earl of Richmond, a Lancaster descendant of Edward III; Married Elizabeth of York to unite both factions as "Tudors"
* Henry VIII	1509 - 1547	Famous for his six wives; Act of Supremacy separated Church of England from Roman Catholicism. Placed severe restrictions on religious plays
Edward VI	1547 - 1553	Protestant son of Henry VIII and Jane Seymour
Jane Grey	1553	Protestant grand-niece of of Henry VIII; Ruled only 14 days
Mary I	1553 - 1558	"Bloody Mary'; Catholic daughter of Henry VIII and Catherine of Aragon
Elizabeth I	1558 - 1603	"Good Queen Bess"; Protestant daughter of Henry VIII and Anne Boleyn

Indicates that a play was written about this ruler by William Shakespeare.

RULERS OF BRITAIN   1603-PRESENT

STUART

James I	1603 - 1625	Son of Mary Queen of Scots (the Catholic grand-niece of Henry VIII); . James VI of Scotland becomes James I of <u>Great Britain.</u> Brought great interest in the masque type of play
Charles I	1625 - 1649	Ruled during Thirty Years War (1618-1648); Beheaded by the Puritans

COMMONWEALTH

Oliver Cromwell	1653 - 1658	"Lord Protector"; Oversees destruction of the theatres and scripts
Richard Cromwell	1658 - 1659	Resigned after one year as the second "Lord Protector"

RESTORATION OF THE STUARTS

Charles II	1660 - 1685	Pro-Catholic second son of Charles I; Brought French style plays to England during "The Restoration"
James II	1685 - 1688	Catholic third son of Charles I; Deposed in 1688; the last Catholic ruler of England. Brief period of "Interregnum" ("between reigns") 1688-1689
William III	1689 - 1702	"Of Orange"; Protestant son of William, Prince of Orange, and Mary Stuart, daughter of Charles I.
& Mary II	1689 - 1694	William's wife, oldest daughter of James II. (William and Mary were first cousins as both were grandchildren of Charles I.)
Anne	1702 - 1714	Mary's sister; second daughter of James II

HANOVER

George I	1714 - 1727	Son of Ernest, Elector of Hanover, and Sophia, granddaughter of James I
George II	1727 - 1760	German prince, but absorbed the English culture that his father had not
George III	1760 - 1820	Grandson of George II; Ruled during the American Revolution
George IV	1820 - 1830	Was Prince Regent from 1811-1820
William IV	1830 - 1837	Third son of George III
Victoria	1837 - 1901	Niece of George IV and William IV; Ruled Great Britain for 63 years

SAXE-COBURG AND GOTHA

Edward VII	1901 - 1910	Eldest son of Queen Victoria; took the family name of his father, Prince Albert

WINDSOR

George V	1910 - 1936	Second son of Edward VII; Changed the royal surname to Windsor during the first World War after a German aircraft "Gotha" bombed London.
Edward VIII	1936	Abdicated the throne after 11 months to wed American divorcee Mrs. Wallis Simpson.
George VI	1936 -1952	Second son of George V
Elizabeth II	1952-Present	Eldest daughter of George V; Married Philip Mountbatten, prince of Greece and Denmark; Four children Charles (Prince of Wales); Anne (The Princess Royal); Andrew (Duke of York); and Edward (Earl of Wessex). Her eldest son, Charles, will succeed her. If Charles should pre-decease his mother, the queen's successor would be William, the elder son of the Prince of Wales.

THE ELIZABETHAN ERA

The Renaissance came to England under the reign of Queen Elizabeth I (1533-1603), the second daughter of King Henry VIII. After the execution of her Catholic rival Mary Stuart in 1587 and the defeat of the Spanish Armada in 1588, England was free from external and internal wars for the first time in hundreds of years. This new political and religious stability allowed arts and literature to thrive.

Prior to this time, actors were considered vagrants and vagabonds and were often arrested. No public theatres were allowed within the city limits of London. During Queen Elizabeth's reign, acting troupes were licensed and most were under the patronage of a wealthy noble, which gave actors a higher financial stability and social status).

Queen Elizabeth, aware of how her father had used theatre to influence the masses, forbade all plays dealing with religious and political topics. All plays required the Crown's approval before public performances, which led to the traditions of final dress rehearsals (with invited audience) and opening nights.

ELIZABETHAN PLAYWRIGHTS (Shakespeare's Contemporaries)

Thomas Kyd (1558-1594) wrote one of the most popular play of the 1500s, ***The Spanish Tragedy***, the first surviving "Revenge play."

John Lyly (1554-1606) wrote pastoral comedies such as ***Love's Metamorphosis*** for children's companies

Robert Greene (1560-1592) wrote pastoral comedies for adult companies.

Christopher Marlowe (1564-1593) was a playwright with a stature nearly equal to Shakespeare's. He was killed in a tavern brawl in 1593, but his killers were acquitted on the grounds of self-defense. His plays include ***Tamburlaine the Great, The Jew of Malta***, ***Edward II*** and ***Dr. Faustus***, which has been retold in countless stories, novels, plays, ballets, operas and films.

Ben Jonson (1572-1637) is considered the greatest Elizabethan playwright after Shakespeare and is best known for his comedies: ***Volpone, The Alchemist*** and ***Bartholmew Fair.*** He wrote many court masques for King James I and was awarded a royal pension in 1616, making him England's first Poet Laureate.

WILLIAM SHAKESPEARE

William Shakespeare (April 23, 1564 - April 23, 1616) is widely considered to be the greatest dramatist of all time. Born in Stratford, he received a good grammar school education, but did not attend college (as he was often reminded by his contemporaries).

In 1571, at the age of 18, Shakespeare married 26 year-old Anne Hathaway. Their first child, Susanna, was born five months later. (Illegitimacy was not uncommon in the 1500s.) In 1585, their twins were born. The boy, Hamnet, died at the age of 11; the daughter, Judith, lived to the age of 77. Their eldest child, Susanna, lived to the age of 66.

Between 1585 and 1592, it is thought that Shakespeare left his family in Stratford to join an acting company. In 1592, a pamphlet by Robert Greene called Shakespeare an "upstart crow" who borrows plots for his own plays. (This established that Shakespeare was making a name for himself as a playwright in London by 1592.)

James Burbage built **The Theatre**, the first public theatre in a northeast suburb of London in 1576. Within 20 years, two other theatres, **The Curtain** and **The Rose**, were also prominent. Shakespeare joined Burbage's acting company, the Lord Chamberlain's Men in 1594 and remained with the company as an actor, writer and part owner of **The Globe Theatre** for the rest of his career.

Scholars traditionally attribute 37 plays to Shakespeare, although they often disagree in determining in which order they were written. Before joining the Lord Chamberlain's Men in 1594, Shakespeare is believed to have written the following:

> **COMEDIES**: *The Comedy of Errors, Two Gentlemen of Verona, The Taming of the Shrew*
> **TRAGEDIES**: *Titus Andronicus*
> **HISTORIES**: *Henry VI (parts 1, 2 and 3), Richard III*

Shakespeare is believed to have written the following during his early years at **The Theatre** between 1594 and 1599:

> **COMEDIES**: *Love's Labour's Lost, A Midsummer Night's Dream, The Merchant of Venice, Much Ado About Nothing, As You Like It*
> **TRAGEDIES**: *Romeo & Juliet, Julius Caesar*
> **HISTORIES**: *Richard II, King John, Henry IV (parts 1 and 2), Henry V*

In 1599 Burbage's lease expired at The Theatre. The company dismantled their building, transported it south of the Thames River, and renamed it **The Globe Theatre**. Shakespeare is believed to have written the following between 1599 and 1608:

> **COMEDIES**: *Twelfth Night, Merry Wives of Windsor, Troilus & Cressida, All's Well That Ends Well, Measure For Measure*
> **TRAGEDIES**: *Hamlet, Othello, King Lear, Macbeth, Antony & Cleopatra, Coriolanus, Timon of Athens*

In 1608, King James I allowed Burbage's company, now called The King's Company (or The King's Men after the death of Queen Elizabeth), to perform at the indoor **Blackfriar's Theatre** during the winter months. Shakespeare is believed to have written the following between 1608 and 1613:

> **COMEDIES**: *Pericles, Cymbeline, A Winter's Tale, The Tempest*
> **HISTORIES**: *Henry VIII*

The Globe Theatre burned in 1613 during the first performance of *Henry VIII*. The Globe was immediately rebuilt in 1613, but torn down in 1644. The Globe was rebuilt in the 1990s, and opened as a functioning Elizabethan theatre in 1997.

Shakespeare retired to Stratford, where he died in 1616. His widow, Anne Hathaway, died in 1623. That same year, actors John Heminges and Henry Condell published **The First Folio,** a collection of 36 of Shakespeare's 37 plays.

THE GLOBE THEATRE was typical of Elizabethan structures, roughly circular in shape, and open to the sky. Plays were performed during the daylight hours of the summer months. There was no scenery except a permanent scenic façade. Without stage lighting, all references to the time of day and condition of the weather, and the play's mood and atmosphere, were conveyed by the actor's dialogue. As women were not allowed to perform in the Public Theatre, young men or boys of small physical stature and youthful voices played all women's roles. *This may account for the relatively few women's roles (usually no more than three) in plays by Elizabethan authors.*

NOTABLE FILM VERSIONS OF "A MIDSUMMER NIGHT'S DREAM"

William Shakespeare

1934: Director Max Reinhardt's cast included Mickey Rooney as Puck and James Cagney as Bottom. The film was nominated for a Best Picture Oscar and won two Academy Awards.

1968: Director Peter Hall's cast included Diana Rigg as Helena, Helen Mirren as Hermia, Ian Holm as Puck and Judi Dench as Titania. *(This film is often confused with Peter Brook's 1970 stage version, which popularized the doubling of Theseus/Oberon and Hippolyta/Titania to suggest that the fairy and mortal worlds were mirror versions of each other.)*

1999: Director/Adaptor Michael Hoffman's version updated the setting to the late 1800's. The cast:

THESEUS	David Strathairn
HIPPOLYTA	Sophie Marceau
PHILOSTRATE	John Sessions
EGEUS	Bernard Hill
HELENA	Calista Flockhart
HERMIA	Anna Friel
DEMETRIUS	Christian Bale
LYSANDER	Dominic West
PETER QUINCE	Roger Rees
NICK BOTTOM	Kevin Kline
FRANCIS FLUTE	Sam Rockwell
ROBIN STARVELING	Max Wright
SNUG	Gregory Jbara
TOM SNOUT	Bill Irwin
TITANIA	Michelle Pfeiffer
OBERON	Rupert Everett
PUCK	Stanley Tucci

NOTABLE QUOTES:

The course of true love never did run smooth.
Lysander: I-1

Over hill, over dale.
Fairy: II-1

I know a bank where the wild thyme blows.
Oberon: II-1

Lord, what fools these mortals be!
Puck: III-2

The lunatic, the lover, and the poet
Are of imagination all compact.
Theseus: V-1

The iron tongue of midnight hath told twelve.
Theseus: V-1

If we shadows have offended,
Think but this, and all is mended,
That you have but slumbered here
While these visions did appear.
Puck: V-1

Act 1, Scene 1

Enter Theseus, Hippolyta, Philostrate, with others.

THESEUS
Now, fair Hippolyta, our nuptial hour
Draws on apace. Four happy days bring in
Another moon. But, O, methinks, how slow
This old moon wanes! She lingers my desires,
Like to a step-dame or a dowager   5
Long withering out a young man's revenue.

HIPPOLYTA
Four days will quickly steep themselves in night;
Four nights will quickly dream away the time;
And then the moon, like to a silver bow
New-bent in heaven, shall behold the night   10
Of our solemnities.

THESEUS   Go, Philostrate,
Stir up the Athenian youth to merriments.
Awake the pert and nimble spirit of mirth.
Turn melancholy forth to funerals;   15
The pale companion is not for our pomp.

Philostrate exits.

Hippolyta, I wooed thee with my sword
And won thy love, doing thee injuries,
But I will wed thee in another key,
With pomp, with triumph, and with reveling.   20

*Enter Egeus and his daughter Hermia,
and Lysander and Demetrius*

EGEUS
Happy be Theseus, our renowned duke!

THESEUS
Thanks, good Egeus. What's the news with thee?

EGEUS
Full of vexation come I, with complaint
Against my child, my daughter Hermia.—
Stand forth, Demetrius.—My noble lord,   25
This man hath my consent to marry her.—
Stand forth, Lysander.—And my gracious duke,
This man hath bewitched the bosom of my child.—
Thou, thou, Lysander, thou hast given her rhymes,
And interchanged love-tokens with my child.   30
Thou hast by moonlight at her window sung
With feigning voice verses of feigning love
And stolen the impression of her fantasy
With bracelets of thy hair, rings, gauds, conceits,
Knacks, trifles, nosegays, sweetmeats—messengers   35
Of strong prevailment in unhardened youth:
With cunning hast thou filched my daughter's heart,
Turned her obedience (which is due to me)
To stubborn harshness.— And, my gracious duke,
Be it so she will not here before your Grace   40
Consent to marry with Demetrius,
I beg the ancient privilege of Athens:
As she is mine, I may dispose of her.
Which shall be either to this gentleman
Or to her death, according to our law   45
Immediately provided in that case.

THESEUS
What say you, Hermia? Be advised fair maid.
To you, your father should be as a god,
One that composed your beauties, yea, and one
To whom you are but as a form in wax   50
By him imprinted, and within his power

A MIDSUMMER NIGHT'S DREAM
Act 1. Scene 1

1. our nuptial hour: the time for our wedding
2. draws on apace: draws near
4. lingers: delays

5-6. dowager... revenue: a widow using up the inheritance that will go to her late husband's son when she dies
7. steep themselves: be absorbed by

11. solemnities: ceremonies

17-18. Hippolyta...sword: Theseus captured Hippolyta during a battle against the Amazons.

20. triumph: public celebration

32. feigning voice: a voice singing softly; **feigning love:** pretended love
33. stolen...fantasy: craftily made her imagine you to be the object of her affection
34. gauds: clever gifts, showy things; **conceits:** trinkets
35. Knacks: knickknacks; **nosegays:** flowers
36. prevailment: influence; **unhardened:** inexperienced and therefore impressionable

40. Be it so: if it be so

44. this gentleman: Demetrius

46. Immediately: expressly

47. Be advised: think carefully

To leave the figure or disfigure it.
Demetrius is a worthy gentleman.

HERMIA
So is Lysander.

THESEUS   In himself he is,   55
But in this kind, wanting your father's voice,
The other must be held the worthier.

HERMIA
I would my father looked but with my eyes.

THESEUS
Rather your eyes must with his judgment look.

HERMIA
I do entreat your grace to pardon me.   60
I know not by what power I am made bold,
Nor how it may concern my modesty
In such a presence here to plead my thoughts;
But I beseech your grace that I may know
The worst that may befall me in this case   65
If I refuse to wed Demetrius.

THESEUS
Either to die the death, or to abjure
For ever the society of men.
Therefore, fair Hermia, question your desires,
Know of your youth, examine well your blood,   70
Whether (if you yield not to your father's choice)
You can endure the livery of a nun,
For aye to be in shady cloister mewed,
To live a barren sister all your life,
Chanting faint hymns to the cold fruitless moon.   75
Thrice-blessèd they that master so their blood
To undergo such maiden pilgrimage,
But earthlier happy is the rose distilled
Than that which, withering on the virgin thorn,
Grows, lives and dies in single blessedness.   80

HERMIA
So will I grow, so live, so die, my lord,
Ere I will my virgin patent up
Unto his lordship, whose unwishèd yoke
My soul consents not to give sovereignty.

THESEUS
Take time to pause; and, by the next new moon   85
(The sealing-day betwixt my love and me
For everlasting bond of fellowship),
Upon that day either prepare to die
For disobedience to your father's will,
Or else to wed Demetrius, as he would,   90
Or on Diana's altar to protest
For aye austerity and single life.

DEMETRIUS
Relent, sweet Hermia, and, Lysander, yield
Thy crazèd title to my certain right.

LYSANDER
You have her father's love, Demetrius.   95
Let me have Hermia's. Do you marry him.

EGEUS
Scornful Lysander, true, he hath my love;
And what is mine my love shall render him.
And she is mine, and all my right of her
I do estate unto Demetrius.   100

LYSANDER *[to Theseus]*
I am, my lord, as well derived as he,
As well possessed. My love is more than his;
My fortunes every way as fairly ranked,

52. leave: leave undisturbed or perhaps destroy

56. In this kind: in this case; **wanting ... voice:** without your father's support

62. concern my modesty: affect my reputation

67. die the death: be put to death

70. Know...youth: take in account your age; **blood:** passions, feelings
72. livery of a nun: a nun's distinctive clothing. (Perhaps a Christian nun or a pagan virgin leading a chaste life in the service of the goddess Diana.)
73. For aye: forever; **mewed:** caged (A mew was a cage for hawks.)
75. moon: a symbol of Diana, the goddess of chastity.
77. maiden pilgrimage: chaste life
78-80. But earthlier ... blessedness: but happier is a rose that, though plucked against its will lives on as a perfume than a rose that dies having never been used at all (dies celebate).

82. Ere I...sovereignty: before I give control of my virginity to Demetrius, whom I do not love.

90. as he would: as your father wishes
91. protest: vow
92. austerity: a life of self-denial

94. crazèd title: flawed claim

96. Do you: You

102. well possessed: wealthy

(If not with vantage) as Demetrius';
And (which is more than all these boasts can be) 105
I am beloved of beauteous Hermia.
Why should not I then prosecute my right?
Demetrius, I'll avouch it to his head,
Made love to Nedar's daughter, Helena,
And won her soul; and she, sweet lady, dotes, 110
Devoutly dotes, dotes in idolatry,
Upon this spotted and inconstant man.

THESEUS
I must confess that I have heard so much,
And with Demetrius thought to have spoke thereof;
But, being over-full of self-affairs, 115
My mind did lose it.— But, Demetrius, come,
And come, Egeus; you shall go with me.
I have some private schooling for you both.—
For you, fair Hermia, look you arm yourself
To fit your fancies to your father's will, 120
Or else the law of Athens yields you up
(Which by no means we may extenuate)
To death, or to a vow of single life.—
Come, my Hippolyta. What cheer, my love?
Demetrius and Egeus, go along. 125
I must employ you in some business
Against our nuptial and confer with you
Of something nearly that concerns yourselves.

EGEUS
With duty and desire we follow you.

All but Hermia and Lysander exit.

LYSANDER
How now, my love? Why is your cheek so pale? 130
How chance the roses there do fade so fast?

HERMIA
Belike for want of rain, which I could well
Beteem them from the tempest of my eyes.

LYSANDER
Ay me! For aught that I could ever read,
Could ever hear by tale or history, 135
The course of true love never did run smooth.
But, either it was different in blood,—

HERMIA
O cross! Too high to be enthralled to low.

LYSANDER
Or else misgraffèd in respect of years,—

HERMIA
O spite! Too old to be engaged to young. 140

LYSANDER
Or else it stood upon the choice of friends,—

HERMIA
O hell, to choose love by another's eyes.

LYSANDER
Or, if there were a sympathy in choice,
War, death, or sickness did lay siege to it,
Making it momentany as a sound, 145
Swift as a shadow, short as any dream,
Brief as the lightning in the collied night,
That, in a spleen, unfolds both heaven and earth,
And ere a man hath power to say "Behold!"
The jaws of darkness do devour it up. 150
So quick bright things come to confusion.

104. with vantage: even more (than his)

108. avouch ... head: say it to his face
109. Made love to: courted

112. spotted: marked as having low morals

115. self-affairs: personal business

119. arm: prepare

122. by no means we may extenuate: not even I, as the Duke, may change the law
124. What cheer ... ?: how are you feeling?

127. Against: in preparation for
128. nearly that concerns yourselves: that closely concerns you

132. Belike: most likely
132-133. well beteem: easily give

134. For aught: according to anything

137. different in blood: unequal in social class

138. cross: bar, barrier, obstruction

139. misgraffèd ... years: with a large age difference

141. stood upon: depended on

143. if... choice: if the couples were suitably matched

145. momentany: lasting only a moment; fleeting

147. collied: coal-black
148. in a spleen: suddenly, impulsively; **unfolds:** reveals
149. ere: before
151. confusion: an end, defeat

HERMIA
If then true lovers have been ever crossed,
It stands as an edict in destiny.
Then let us teach our trial patience
Because it is a customary cross,   155
As due to love as thoughts and dreams and sighs,
Wishes and tears, poor Fancy's followers.

LYSANDER
A good persuasion. Therefore, hear me, Hermia:
I have a widow aunt, a dowager
Of great revenue, and she hath no child.   160
From Athens is her house remote seven leagues,
And she respects me as her only son.
There, gentle Hermia, may I marry thee;
And to that place the sharp Athenian law
Cannot pursue us. If thou lovest me then   165
Steal forth thy father's house tomorrow night,
And in the wood, a league without the town
(Where I did meet thee once with Helena,
To do observance to a morn of May)
There will I stay for thee.   170

HERMIA   My good Lysander,
I swear to thee, by Cupid's strongest bow,
By his best arrow with the golden head,
By the simplicity of Venus' doves,
By that which knitteth souls and prospers loves,   175
And by that fire which burned the Carthage queen,
When the false Trojan under sail was seen,
By all the vows that ever men have broke
(In number more than ever women spoke),
In that same place thou hast appointed me,   180
Tomorrow truly will I meet with thee.

LYSANDER
Keep promise, love. Look, here comes Helena.

Enter Helena.

HERMIA
God speed fair Helena. Whither away?

HELENA
Call you me "fair"? That "fair" again unsay.
Demetrius loves your fair. O happy fair!   185
Your eyes are lodestars and your tongue's sweet air
More tunable than lark to shepherd's ear,
When wheat is green, when hawthorn buds appear.
Sickness is catching. O, were favor so!
Yours would I catch, fair Hermia, ere I go.   190
My ear should catch your voice, my eye your eye;
My tongue should catch your tongue's sweet
    melody.
Were the world mine, Demetrius being bated,
The rest I'd give to be to you translated.   195
O, teach me how you look, and with what art
You sway the motion of Demetrius' heart.

HERMIA
I frown upon him, yet he loves me still.

HELENA
O that your frowns would teach my smiles such
    skill!   200

HERMIA
I give him curses, yet he gives me love.

HELENA
O that my prayers could such affection move!

HERMIA
The more I hate, the more he follows me.

152. ever crossed: always hindered

157. Fancy's: Love's

158. A good persuasion: a good point of view for us to take

167. without: outside of

169. To do ... May: to celebrate May Day

176-77. that fire ... was seen: Dido, queen of Carthage burned herself to death after Aeneas, **the false Trojan,** abandoned her by sailing off

183. God speed: a common greeting

185. your fair: your beauty; **happy:** fortunate
186. lodestars: stars that sailors used as guides
187. tunable: melodious
189. favor: looks

194-95. Demetrius ... translated: I'd give the whole world, except for Demetrius, in order to be transformed into you.

HELENA
The more I love, the more he hateth me.

HERMIA
His folly, Helena, is no fault of mine.   205

HELENA
None, but your beauty. Would that fault were mine!

HERMIA
Take comfort: he no more shall see my face.
Lysander and myself will fly this place.
Before the time I did Lysander see,
Seemed Athens as a paradise to me.   210
O, then, what graces in my love do dwell
That he hath turned a heaven unto a hell!

LYSANDER
Helen, to you our minds we will unfold.
Tomorrow night, when Phoebe doth behold
Her silver visage in the watery glass,   215
Decking with liquid pearl the bladed grass
(A time that lovers' flights doth still conceal),
Through Athens' gates have we devised to steal.

HERMIA
And in the wood, where often you and I
Upon faint primrose-beds were wont to lie,   220
Emptying our bosoms of their counsel sweet,
There my Lysander and myself shall meet,
And thence from Athens turn away our eyes
To seek new friends and stranger companies.
Farewell, sweet playfellow. Pray thou for us,   225
And good luck grant thee thy Demetrius.—
Keep word, Lysander. We must starve our sight
From lovers' food till morrow deep midnight.

LYSANDER
I will, my Hermia.
                    Hermia exits.
              Helena, adieu: 230
As you on him, Demetrius dote on you!
                    Lysander exits.

HELENA
How happy some o'er other some can be!
Through Athens I am thought as fair as she.
But what of that? Demetrius thinks not so.
He will not know what all but he do know.   235
And, as he errs, doting on Hermia's eyes,
So I, admiring of his qualities.
Things base and vile, holding no quantity,
Love can transpose to form and dignity.
Love looks not with the eyes, but with the mind;   240
And therefore is winged Cupid painted blind:
Nor hath Love's mind of any judgement taste;
Wings, and no eyes figure unheedy haste.
And therefore is Love said to be a child
Because in choice he is so oft beguiled.   245
As waggish boys in game themselves forswear,
So the boy Love is perjured everywhere.
For, ere Demetrius looked on Hermia's eyne,
He hailed down oaths that he was only mine;
And when this hail some heat from Hermia felt,   250
So he dissolved, and showers of oaths did melt.
I will go tell him of fair Hermia's flight.
Then to the wood will he tomorrow night
Pursue her. And for this intelligence
If I have thanks, it is a dear expense.   255
But herein mean I to enrich my pain,
To have his sight thither and back again.
                                        She exits.

211. what graces ... dwell: how much beauty is in Lysander

214. Phoebe: goddess of the moon (Phoebe is another name for Diana.)
215. wat'ry glass: water reflecting the moon like a mirror
217. still: always

224. stranger companies: the company of strangers

228. lovers' food: the sight of each other

237. So I: so I err
238. holding no quantity: greatly out of proportion

240-47. Love... everywhere: Helena uses the ways that Cupid is often pictured (a blind boy with wings) to describe the qualities of love: blind, without judgment, foolish and inconstant.

254. intelligence: information
255. dear: high priced

Act 1, Scene 2

*Enter Quince the carpenter, and Snug the joiner,
and Bottom the Weaver, and Flute the bellows-mender,
and Snout the tinker, and Starveling the tailor.*

QUINCE Is all our company here?

BOTTOM You were best to call them generally, man by
man, according to the scrip.

QUINCE Here is the scroll of every man's name, which
is thought fit, through all Athens, to play in our   5
interlude before the duke and the duchess, on his
wedding-day at night.

BOTTOM First, good Peter Quince, say what the play
treats on, then read the names of the actors, and
so grow to a point.   10

QUINCE Marry, our play is, "The most lamentable
comedy, and most cruel death of Pyramus and
Thisbe."

BOTTOM A very good piece of work, I assure you, and
a merry. Now, good Peter Quince, call forth your   15
actors by the scroll. Masters, spread yourselves.

QUINCE Answer as I call you. Nick Bottom, the weaver.

BOTTOM Ready. Name what part I am for, and
proceed.

QUINCE You, Nick Bottom, are set down for Pyramus.   20

BOTTOM What is Pyramus--a lover, or a tyrant?

QUINCE A lover, that kills himself most gallant for love.

BOTTOM That will ask some tears in the true performing
of it: if I do it, let the audience look to their eyes;
I will move storms, I will condole in some measure.   25
To the rest: yet my chief humor is for a tyrant:
I could play Ercles rarely, or a part to tear a
cat in, to make all split.
    The raging rocks
    And shivering shocks   30
    Shall break the locks
    Of prison gates;
    And Phibbus' car
    Shall shine from far
    And make and mar   35
    The foolish Fates.
This was lofty! Now name the rest of the players.
This is Ercles' vein, a tyrant's vein; a lover is
more condoling.

QUINCE Francis Flute, the bellows-mender.   40

FLUTE Here, Peter Quince.

QUINCE Flute, you must take Thisby on you.

FLUTE What is Thisby—a wandering knight?

QUINCE It is the lady that Pyramus must love.

FLUTE Nay, faith, let me not play a woman;   45
I have a beard coming.

QUINCE That's all one. You shall play it in a mask,
and you may speak as small as you will.

BOTTOM An I may hide my face, let me play Thisby too.
I'll speak in a monstrous little voice. "Thisne,   50
Thisne!"— "Ah, Pyramus, lover dear! Thy Thisbe
dear, and lady dear!"

QUINCE No, no; you must play Pyramus: and, Flute,
you Thisby.

BOTTOM Well, proceed.   55

**A MIDSUMMER NIGHT'S DREAM
Act 1. Scene 2**

0. joiner: cabinetmaker

2. You were best: you had better; **generally:**
Bottom's mistake for "individually" *(Bottom uses language
oddly and often incorrectly, but his meaning is generally
clear. It was common practice to give rustics comic dialogue
containing linguistic errors and malapropisms)*
  4. which: who
  6. interlude: an entertainment that is performed
between other events

10. grow to a point: apparently "come to a conclusion"
11. Marry: indeed (a common exclamation)
12-13. Pyramus and Thisbe: The story of Pyramus
and Thisbe (very much like that of Romeo and Juliet) is told
in Ovid's *Metamorphoses.*

23. ask: require

25. condole: grieve, lament
26. humor: preference
27. Ercles: Hercules
27-28. tear a cat: rant and rave

33. Phibbus' car: the chariot of the sun god, Phoebus
Apollo

38. Ercles' vein: in the style of Hercules

43. wand'ring knight: heroic knight-errant

47. all one: doesn't matter
48. small: high-pitched, dainty

50. monstrous little: extremely small (Bottom often
uses oxymoronic expressions)

QUINCE Robin Starveling, the tailor.

STARVELING Here, Peter Quince.

QUINCE Robin Starveling, you must play Thisby's mother. Tom Snout, the tinker.

SNOUT Here, Peter Quince. 60

QUINCE You, Pyramus' father. —Myself, Thisbe's father. —Snug, the joiner; you, the lion's part.— And I hope here is a play fitted.

SNUG Have you the lion's part written? Pray you, if it be, give it me, for I am slow of study. 65

QUINCE You may do it extempore, for it is nothing but roaring.

BOTTOM Let me play the lion too: I will roar, that I will do any man's heart good to hear me; I will roar, that I will make the duke say "Let him roar again. Let him roar again!" 70

QUINCE An you should do it too terribly, you would fright the duchess and the ladies, that they would shriek; and that were enough to hang us all.

ALL That would hang us, every mother's son. 75

BOTTOM I grant you, friends, if that you should fright the ladies out of their wits, they would have no more discretion but to hang us: but I will aggravate my voice so that I will roar you as gently as any sucking dove; I will roar you an 'twere any nightingale. 80

QUINCE You can play no part but Pyramus; for Pyramus is a sweet-faced man; a proper man, as one shall see in a summer's day, a most lovely gentleman-like man: therefore you must needs play Pyramus. 85

BOTTOM Well, I will undertake it. What beard were I best to play it in?

QUINCE Why, what you will.

BOTTOM I will discharge it in either your straw-color beard, your orange-tawny beard, your purple-in-grain beard, or your French-crown-color beard, your perfit yellow. 90

QUINCE Some of your French crowns have no hair at all, and then you will play barefaced. But, masters, here are your parts *(giving out the parts)*: and I am to entreat you, request you and desire you, to con them by tomorrow night; and meet me in the palace wood, a mile without the town, by moonlight. There will we rehearse, for if we meet in the city, we shall be dogged with company, and our devices known. In the meantime I will draw a bill of properties, such as our play wants. I pray you, fail me not. 95 / 100

BOTTOM We will meet; and there we may rehearse most obscenely and courageously. Take pains; be perfit: adieu. 105

QUINCE At the duke's oak we meet.

BOTTOM Enough. Hold or cut bowstrings.

They exit.

72. terribly: fiercely

74. were: would be

78. discretion: choice; **aggravate:** Bottom's mistake for "moderate" or "modulate"
79. roar you: roar for you
79-80. sucking dove: Bottom means a hatchling or "sitting" dove, but uses the term "sucking" as in an unweaned mammal.
80. an 'twere: as if it were
82. proper: handsome

89. discharge: perform

92. perfit: perfect

93-94. French ... all: an allusion to syphilis (the "French disease") and the baldness caused by it

96. con: learn

98. without: outside of

100. devices: plans
101. bill of properties: list of stage props

104. obscenely: Bottom may mean "seemly".
105. perfit: perfectly memorized

Act 2, Scene 1

*Enter a Fairy at one door and
Robin Goodfellow at another.*

ROBIN
How now, spirit? Whither wander you?

FAIRY
  Over hill, over dale,
    Thorough bush, thorough brier,
  Over park, over pale,
    Thorough flood, thorough fire;   5
  I do wander everywhere,
  Swifter than the moon's sphere.
  And I serve the Fairy Queen,
  To dew her orbs upon the green.
  The cowslips tall her pensioners be;   10
  In their gold coats spots you see;
  Those be rubies, fairy favors;
  In those freckles live their savors.
I must go seek some dewdrops here
And hang a pearl in every cowslip's ear.   15
Farewell, thou lob of spirits; I'll be gone.
Our queen and all our elves come here anon.

ROBIN
The King doth keep his revels here tonight.
Take heed the Queen come not within his sight,
For Oberon is passing fell and wrath   20
Because that she, as her attendant, hath
A lovely boy, stolen from an Indian king;
She never had so sweet a changeling.
And jealous Oberon would have the child
Knight of his train, to trace the forests wild.   25
But she perforce withholds the loved boy,
Crowns him with flowers, and makes him all her
  joy.
And now they never meet in grove or green,
By fountain clear, or spangled starlight sheen,   30
But they do square, that all their elves for fear
Creep into acorn-cups and hide them there.

FAIRY
Either I mistake your shape and making quite,
Or else you are that shrewd and knavish sprite
Called Robin Goodfellow. Are not you he   35
That frights the maidens of the villagery,
Skim milk, and sometimes labor in the quern
And bootless make the breathless housewife churn,
And sometime make the drink to bear no barm,
Mislead night-wanderers, laughing at their harm?   40
Those that "Hobgoblin" call you and "sweet Puck,"
You do their work, and they shall have good luck.
Are not you he?

ROBIN   Thou speakest aright.
I am that merry wanderer of the night.   45
I jest to Oberon and make him smile
When I a fat and bean-fed horse beguile,
Neighing in likeness of a filly foal.
And sometime lurk I in a gossip's bowl
In very likeness of a roasted crab,   50
And when she drinks, against her lips I bob
And on her withered dewlap pour the ale.
The wisest aunt, telling the saddest tale,
Sometime for three-foot stool mistaketh me;
Then slip I from her bum, down topples she,   55
And 'Tailor' cries, and falls into a cough,
And then the whole quire hold their hips and loffe,
And waxen in their mirth and neeze and swear

107. Hold, or cut bowstrings: Stand by your word or be disgraced.
A MIDSUMMER NIGHT'S DREAM
Act 2. Scene 1

0. Robin Goodfellow: a "puck," or mischievous spirit

3. Thorough: through

9. orbs: circles (referring to a circle of darker, thicker grass in a meadow that was called a "fairy ring" and was thought to be caused by dancing fairies)

16. lob: oaf, lout
17. anon: soon

18. revels: special celebration

20. passing: extremely; **fell and wrath:** fiercely angry

25. trace: travel through
26. perforce: with force

29. they: Oberon and Titania

31. square: argue

37. Skim milk: steal the cream from the milk; **labor in the quern:** work at the quern (a small mill) to make difficult
38. bootless ... churn: make her churning produce no butter; **bootless:** fruitlessly
39. barm: the head on beer.

47. beguile: deceive, trick

49. gossip's bowl: the cup from which the gossiping woman is drinking
50. crab: crab apple
52. dewlap: the fold of skin hanging from the neck of certain animals

57. quire: company
57-58. loffe ... waxen ... neeze: "laugh," "wax" (increase), "sneeze"

A merrier hour was never wasted there.
But, room, fairy. Here comes Oberon. 60

FAIRY
And here my mistress. Would that he were gone!

Enter OBERON, the King of the Fairies at one door,
with his train, and TITANIA, the Queen at another, with hers.

OBERON
Ill met by moonlight, proud Titania.

TITANIA
What, jealous Oberon? Fairies, skip hence.
I have forsworn his bed and company.

OBERON
Tarry, rash wanton. Am not I thy lord? 65

TITANIA
Then I must be thy lady. But I know
When thou hast stolen away from Fairyland
And in the shape of Corin sat all day
Playing on pipes of corn and versing love
To amorous Phillida. Why art thou here, 70
Come from the farthest Steppe of India,
But that, forsooth, the bouncing Amazon,
Your buskined mistress and your warrior love,
To Theseus must be wedded, and you come
To give their bed joy and prosperity. 75

OBERON
How canst thou thus for shame, Titania,
Glance at my credit with Hippolyta,
Knowing I know thy love to Theseus?
Didst thou not lead him through the glimmering
  night 80
From Perigouna, whom he ravishèd?
And make him with fair Aegles break his faith,
With Ariadne and Antiopa?

TITANIA
These are the forgeries of jealousy;
And never, since the middle summer's spring, 85
Met we on hill, in dale, forest, or mead,
By pavèd fountain or by rushy brook,
Or in the beached margent of the sea,
To dance our ringlets to the whistling wind,
But with thy brawls thou hast disturbed our sport. 90
Therefore the winds, piping to us in vain,
As in revenge, have sucked up from the sea
Contagious fogs, which falling in the land,
Have every pelting river made so proud
That they have overborne their continents. 95
The ox hath therefore stretched his yoke in vain,
The plowman lost his sweat, and the green corn
Hath rotted ere his youth attained a beard.
The fold stands empty in the drownèd field,
And crows are fatted with the murrain flock. 100
The nine men's-morris is filled up with mud,
And the quaint mazes in the wanton green,
For lack of tread, are undistinguishable.
The human mortals want their winter here.
No night is now with hymn or carol blessed. 105
Therefore the moon, the governess of floods,
Pale in her anger, washes all the air,
That rheumatic diseases do abound.
And thorough this distemperature we see
The seasons alter: hoary-headed frosts 110
Far in the fresh lap of the crimson rose,
And on old Hiems' thin and icy crown
An odorous chaplet of sweet summer buds

60. room: make room, stand aside

64. forsworn: formally rejected

65. lord: husband (and therefore rightfully having control over his wife)
66. lady: wife (and therefore having the right to expect faithfulness from her husband)
68. in … Corin: disguised as a lovesick shepherd
69. of corn: wheat straws
70. Phillida: mythical shepherdess of love poetry
71. Steppe: extensive sloping plain
72. forsooth: in truth; **bouncing Amazon:** Hippolyta
73. buskined: booted

77. Glance at: allude to; **credit:** reputation

81-83. Perigouna…Aegles…Arladne…Antiopa: Lovers whom Theseus deserted

85. middle summer's spring: the beginning of midsummer
86. mead: meadow
87. pavèd: pebbled
88. margent: margin
89. ringlets: circle dances

91. piping: whistling

94. pelting: paltry, insignificant
95. continents: river banks

97. green corn : grain

99. fold: sheepfold, or pen
100. murrain flock: sheep dead from murrain, an infectious disease
101. nine-men's-morris: a playing field for a game of the same name
102. quaint: elaborate; **mazes:** intricate interconnecting paths; **wanton green:** thick grass
103. tread: human footsteps which keep a path clear by walking the maze; **undistinguishable:** not perceptible
104. want: lack

112. Hiems': winter's
113. odorous: fragrant

Is, as in mockery, set. The spring, the summer,
The childing autumn, angry winter, change   115
Their wonted liveries, and the mazèd world,
By their increase, now knows not which is which.
And this same progeny of evils comes
From our debate, from our dissension;
We are their parents and original.   120

OBERON
Do you amend it then. It lies in you.
Why should Titania cross her Oberon?
I do but beg a little changeling boy,
To be my henchman.

TITANIA   Set your heart at rest: 125
The Fairyland buys not the child of me.
His mother was a vot'ress of my order,
And in the spicèd Indian air by night,
Full often hath she gossiped by my side
And sat with me on Neptune's yellow sands,   130
Marking the embarkèd traders on the flood,
When we have laughed to see the sails conceive
And grow big-bellied with the wanton wind;
Which she, with pretty and with swimming gait,
Following (her womb then rich with my young   135
     squire,)
Would imitate, and sail upon the land,
To fetch me trifles, and return again,
As from a voyage, rich with merchandise.
But she, being mortal, of that boy did die,   140
And for her sake do I rear up her boy,
And for her sake I will not part with him.

OBERON
How long within this wood intend you stay?

TITANIA
Perchance till after Theseus' wedding-day.
If you will patiently dance in our round   145
And see our moonlight revels, go with us.
If not, shun me, and I will spare your haunts.

OBERON
Give me that boy, and I will go with thee.

TITANIA
Not for thy fairy kingdom. Fairies, away!
We shall chide downright, if I longer stay.   150

               Titania and her fairies exit.

OBERON
Well, go thy way. Thou shalt not from this grove
Till I torment thee for this injury.—
My gentle Puck, come hither. Thou rememb'rest
Since once I sat upon a promontory
And heard a mermaid on a dolphin's back   155
Uttering such dulcet and harmonious breath
That the rude sea grew civil at her song
And certain stars shot madly from their spheres
To hear the sea-maid's music.

ROBIN   I remember.   160

OBERON
That very time I saw (but thou couldst not),
Flying between the cold moon and the earth,
Cupid all armed. A certain aim he took
At a fair vestal thronèd by the west,
And loosed his love-shaft smartly from his bow   165
As it should pierce a hundred thousand hearts.
But I might see young Cupid's fiery shaft
Quenched in the chaste beams of the watery moon,

115. childing: child-producing fruitful; **change:** swap
116. wonted liveries: usual outfits; **mazèd:** bewildered
118-19. this same...debate: these evils are the offspring of our quarrel
120. original: origin

122. cross: resist

124. henchman: page, squire

127. vot'ress ... order: woman vowed to serve me

130. Neptune: the god of the sea
131. Marking: watching; **embarkèd...flood:** merchant ships on the ocean
133. wanton: lewd or possibly playful

145. round: circle dance

147. spare your haunts: avoid the places you commonly go

150. chide: fight; **downright:** outright

151. from: leave
152. injury: insult

154. Since: when

164. vestal: virgin (Perhaps referring to Queen Elizabeth I.)

167. might: could

And the imperial vot'ress passèd on,
In maiden meditation, fancy-free.   170
Yet marked I where the bolt of Cupid fell:
It fell upon a little western flower,
Before, milk-white, now purple with love's wound,
And maidens call it "love-in-idleness."
Fetch me that flower; the herb I showed thee once.   175
The juice of it on sleeping eyelids laid
Will make or man or woman madly dote
Upon the next live creature that it sees.
Fetch me this herb; and be thou here again
Ere the leviathan can swim a league.   180

ROBIN
I'll put a girdle round about the earth
In forty minutes.

He exits.

OBERON   Having once this juice,
I'll watch Titania when she is asleep
And drop the liquor of it in her eyes.   185
The next thing then she, waking, looks upon,
(Be it on lion, bear, or wolf, or bull,
On meddling monkey, or on busy ape)
She shall pursue it with the soul of love.
And ere I take this charm from off her sight,   190
(As I can take it with another herb),
I'll make her render up her page to me.
But who comes here? I am invisible;
And I will overhear their conference.

Enter Demetrius, Helena following him.

DEMETRIUS
I love thee not; therefore pursue me not.   195
Where is Lysander and fair Hermia?
The one I'll stay; the other stayeth me.
Thou told'st me they were stol'n unto this wood;
And here am I, and wood within this wood
Because I cannot meet my Hermia.   200
Hence, get thee gone, and follow me no more.

HELENA
You draw me, you hard-hearted adamant!
But yet you draw not iron, for my heart
Is true as steel. Leave you your power to draw,
And I shall have no power to follow you.   205

DEMETRIUS
Do I entice you? Do I speak you fair?
Or rather do I not in plainest truth
Tell you I do not, nor I cannot love you?

HELENA
And even for that do I love you the more.
I am your spaniel, and, Demetrius,   210
The more you beat me I will fawn on you.
Use me but as your spaniel: spurn me, strike me,
Neglect me, lose me; only give me leave,
(Unworthy as I am) to follow you.
What worser place can I beg in your love   215
(And yet a place of high respect with me)
Than to be usèd as you use your dog?

DEMETRIUS
Tempt not too much the hatred of my spirit,
For I am sick when I do look on thee.

HELENA
And I am sick when I look not on you.   220

169. imperial: commanding, majestic; **vot'ress:** a woman under a vow (most likely a vow of chastity)
171. bolt: arrow

175. herb: plant

180. leviathan: a monstrous sea creature; **league:** approximately three miles

183. juice: nectar from the flower

192. page: servant boy

197. stay: stop; **stayeth:** holds

199. and wood: and insane

202. adamant: magnet
203. draw: attract
204. Leave you: abandon

206. speak you fair: speak civilly to you

DEMETRIUS
You do impeach your modesty too much
To leave the city and commit yourself
Into the hands of one that loves you not,
To trust the opportunity of night
And the ill counsel of a desert place   225
With the rich worth of your virginity.

HELENA
Your virtue is my privilege. For that
It is not night when I do see your face,
Therefore I think I am not in the night.
Nor doth this wood lack worlds of company,   230
For you, in my respect, are all the world.
Then, how can it be said I am alone
When all the world is here to look on me?

DEMETRIUS
I'll run from thee and hide me in the brakes,
And leave thee to the mercy of wild beasts.   235

HELENA
The wildest hath not such a heart as you.
Run when you will. The story shall be changed:
Apollo flies, and Daphne holds the chase;
The dove pursues the griffin; the mild hind
Makes speed to catch the tiger. Bootless speed   240
When cowardice pursues and valor flies.

DEMETRIUS
I will not stay thy questions. Let me go,
Or, if thou follow me, do not believe
But I shall do thee mischief in the wood.

HELENA
Ay, in the temple, in the town, the field,   245
You do me mischief. Fie, Demetrius!
Your wrongs do set a scandal on my sex.
We cannot fight for love as men may do.
We should be wooed and were not made to woo.
                Demetrius exits.

I'll follow thee and make a heaven of hell,   250
To die upon the hand I love so well.
                Helena exits.

OBERON
Fare thee well, nymph. Ere he do leave this grove,
Thou shalt fly him and he shall seek thy love.
                Enter Robin.

Hast thou the flower there? Welcome, wanderer.

ROBIN
Ay, there it is.   255

OBERON   I pray thee, give it me.
                Robin gives him the flower.

I know a bank where the wild thyme blows,
Where oxlips and the nodding violet grows,
Quite over-canopied with luscious woodbine,
With sweet musk-roses and with eglantine.   260
There sleeps Titania sometime of the night,
Lulled in these flowers with dances and delight;
And there the snake throws her enamelled skin,
Weed wide enough to wrap a fairy in.
And with the juice of this I'll streak her eyes   265
And make her full of hateful fantasies.
Take thou some of it, and seek through this grove.
                He gives Robin part of the flower.

221. impeach: call into question; **modesty:** proper, chaste female behavior

225. ill: evil; **desert:** wild, uninhabited

227. virtue: moral goodness; **privilege:** protection

231. in my respect: from my point of view

234. brakes: thickets

239. hind: female deer
240. Bootless: useless

242. stay: stay for
243-44. do ... But: be certain
244-246. do...mischief: harm

247. my sex: all females

251. upon: by

253. fly: run from

263. throws: casts off
264. Weed: garment

A sweet Athenian lady is in love
With a disdainful youth. Anoint his eyes,
But do it when the next thing he espies   270
May be the lady. Thou shalt know the man
By the Athenian garments he hath on.
Effect it with some care, that he may prove
More fond on her than she upon her love.
And look thou meet me ere the first cock crow.   275

ROBIN
Fear not, my lord, your servant shall do so.

They exit.

Act 2, Scene 2
    Enter Titania, Queen of Fairies, with her train.

TITANIA
Come, now a roundel and a fairy song;
Then, for the third part of a minute, hence—
Some to kill cankers in the musk-rose buds,
Some war with reremice for their leathern wings
To make my small elves coats, and some keep back   5
The clamorous owl that nightly hoots and wonders
At our quaint spirits. Sing me now asleep;
Then to your offices and let me rest.

    She lies down. The Fairies sing.

FIRST FAIRY
You spotted snakes with double tongue,
Thorny hedgehogs, be not seen.   10
Newts and blindworms, do no wrong,
Come not near our Fairy Queen.

CHORUS
Philomel, with melody
Sing in our sweet lullaby.
Lulla, lulla, lullaby, lulla, lulla, lullaby.   15
Never harm,
Nor spell nor charm
Come our lovely lady nigh.
So, good night, with lullaby.

FIRST FAIRY
Weaving spiders, come not here.   20
Hence, you long-legged spinners, hence.
Beetles black, approach not near.
Worm nor snail, do no offence.

CHORUS
Philomel, with melody
Sing in our sweet lullaby.   25
Lulla, lulla, lullaby, lulla, lulla, lullaby.
Never harm,
Nor spell nor charm
Come our lovely lady nigh.
So, good night, with lullaby.   30

    Titania sleeps.

SECOND FAIRY
Hence, away! Now all is well.
One aloof stand sentinel.

    Fairies exit.
    Enter Oberon, who anoints Titania's eyelids with the nectar.

OBERON
What thou seest when thou dost wake,
Do it for thy true love take,
Love and languish for his sake.   35
Be it ounce, or cat, or bear,
Pard, or boar with bristled hair,
In thy eye that shall appear

274. fond on: wildly in love with

A MIDSUMMER NIGHT'S DREAM
Act 2. Scene 2

    1. roundel: a dance in a circle

    3. cankers: worms, grubs
    4. reremice: bats

    7. quaint: dainty
    8. offices: responsibilities

    11. Newts and blindworms: species of salamanders
and reptiles once thought to be poisonous

    13. Philomel: the nightingale

    36. ounce: lynx; **cat:** lion or tiger
    37. Pard: leopard
    38. that: that which

When thou wak'st, it is thy dear:
Wake when some vile thing is near.   40

Oberon exits.
Enter Lysander and Hermia.

LYSANDER
Fair love, you faint with wandering in the wood.
And, to speak troth, I have forgot our way.   **42. troth:** truthfully
We'll rest us, Hermia, if you think it good,
And tarry for the comfort of the day.

HERMIA
Be it so, Lysander. Find you out a bed   45
For I upon this bank will rest my head.

LYSANDER
One turf shall serve as pillow for us both;
One heart, one bed, two bosoms and one troth.   **48. troth:** faithful vow

HERMIA
Nay, good Lysander. For my sake, my dear,
Lie further off yet. Do not lie so near.   50

LYSANDER
O, take the sense, sweet, of my innocence!   **51. take . . . innocence:** please accept the innocent
Love takes the meaning in love's conference.   meaning of what I just said
I mean, that my heart unto yours is knit   **52. Love...conference:** when lovers talk, love hears
So that but one heart we can make of it;   the truer meaning
Two bosoms interchainèd with an oath—   55
So then two bosoms and a single troth.
Then by your side no bed-room me deny
For lying so, Hermia, I do not lie.

HERMIA
Lysander riddles very prettily.
Now much beshrew my manners and my pride   60   **60. beshrew:** curse
If Hermia meant to say Lysander lied.
But, gentle friend, for love and courtesy,
Lie further off; in human modesty.   **63. human:** humane, courteous
Such separation as may well be said,
Becomes a virtuous bachelor and a maid,   65
So far be distant; and, good night, sweet friend.
Thy love ne'er alter till thy sweet life end!

LYSANDER
"Amen, amen", to that fair prayer, say I;
And then end life when I end loyalty!
Here is my bed. Sleep give thee all his rest!   70

HERMIA
With half that wish the wisher's eyes be pressed!
They sleep.
Enter Robin.

ROBIN
Through the forest have I gone,
But Athenian found I none
On whose eyes I might approve   **74. approve:** demonstrate
This flower's force in stirring love.   75
He sees Lysander.

Night and silence! Who is here?
Weeds of Athens he doth wear.   **77. Weeds:** Garments
This is he my master said
Despisèd the Athenian maid.
And here the maiden, sleeping sound,   80
On the dank and dirty ground.
Pretty soul, she durst not lie
Near this lack-love, this kill-courtesy.—
Churl, upon thy eyes I throw
All the power this charm doth owe.   85   **85. owe:** own, have
He anoints Lysander's eyelids with the nectar.

When thou wak'st, let love forbid
Sleep his seat on thy eyelid.
So awake when I am gone,
For I must now to Oberon.

He exits.
Enter Demetrius and Helena, running

HELENA
Stay, though thou kill me, sweet Demetrius.   90

DEMETRIUS
I charge thee, hence, and do not haunt me thus.

91. charge: command

HELENA
O, wilt thou darkling leave me? Do not so.

92. darkling: in the dark

DEMETRIUS
Stay, on thy peril: I alone will go.
Demetrius exits.

HELENA
O, I am out of breath in this fond chase.
The more my prayer, the lesser is my grace.   95
Happy is Hermia, wheresoe'er she lies,
For she hath blessèd and attractive eyes.
How came her eyes so bright? Not with salt tears.
If so, my eyes are oftener washed than hers.
No, no, I am as ugly as a bear,   100
For beasts that meet me run away for fear.
Therefore no marvel though Demetrius
Do as a monster fly my presence thus.
What wicked and dissembling glass of mine
Made me compare with Hermia's sphery eyne?   105
But who is here? Lysander, on the ground!
Dead or asleep? I see no blood, no wound.—
Lysander if you live, good sir, awake.

94. fond: frivolous
95. grace: reward for prayer

103. as: as if I were
104. glass: mirror
105. compare with: rival, vie with; **sphery eyne:** star-like, twinkling eyes

LYSANDER *[waking up]*
And run through fire I will for thy sweet sake.
Transparent Helena! Nature shows art,   110
That through thy bosom makes me see thy heart.
Where is Demetrius? O, how fit a word
Is that vile name to perish on my sword!

110. Transparent: capable of being clearly seen;
Nature shows art: Nature reveals Helena's inner beauty like a magician.

HELENA
Do not say so. Lysander, say not so.
What though he love your Hermia? Lord, what though?   115
Yet Hermia still loves you. Then be content.

LYSANDER
Content with Hermia? No, I do repent
The tedious minutes I with her have spent.
Not Hermia, but Helena I love.   120
Who will not change a raven for a dove?
The will of man is by his reason swayed,
And reason says you are the worthier maid.
Things growing are not ripe until their season;
So I, being young, till now ripe not to reason.   125
And touching now the point of human skill,
Reason becomes the marshal to my will
And leads me to your eyes, where I o'erlook
Love's stories written in love's richest book.

121. change: exchange
122-29. The will... book: Lysander reasons that he has suddenly grown up and with this new maturity he rationally loves Helena. **will:** desire

126. point: the highest point; **skill:** judgment

128. o'erlook: see

HELENA
Wherefore was I to this keen mockery born?   130
When at your hands did I deserve this scorn?
Is't not enough, is't not enough, young man,
That I did never, no, nor never can,
Deserve a sweet look from Demetrius' eye,
But you must flout my insufficiency?   135
Good troth, you do me wrong, good sooth, you do,
In such disdainful manner me to woo.

130. Wherefore: why

136. Good troth, good sooth: in truth

But fare you well. Perforce I must confess
I thought you lord of more true gentleness.
O, that a lady, of one man refused.   140
Should of another therefore be abused!
                                    She exits.

LYSANDER
She sees not Hermia.—Hermia, sleep thou there,
And never mayst thou come Lysander near!
For, as a surfeit of the sweetest things
The deepest loathing to the stomach brings,   145
Or as the heresies that men do leave
Are hated most of those they did deceive,
So thou, my surfeit and my heresy,
Of all be hated, but the most of me!
And, all my powers, address your love and might   150
To honor Helen and to be her knight.
                                    He exits.

HERMIA *[waking up]*
Help me, Lysander, help me! Do thy best
To pluck this crawling serpent from my breast.
Ay me, for pity! What a dream was here!
Lysander, look how I do quake with fear.   155
Methought a serpent eat my heart away,
And you sat smiling at his cruel prey.
Lysander! What, removed? Lysander, lord!
What, out of hearing? Gone? No sound, no word?
Alack, where are you? Speak, an if you hear;   160
Speak, of all loves! I swoon almost with fear.—
No? Then I well perceive you all not nigh
Either death or you I'll find immediately.
                                    She exits.

Act 3, Scene 1
          With Titania still asleep on stage, enter the Clowns,
          Quince, Snug, Bottom, Flute, Snout, and Starveling

BOTTOM Are we all met?

QUINCE Pat, pat. And here's a marvellous convenient
     place for our rehearsal. This green plot shall be
     our stage, this hawthorn-brake our tiring-house;
     and we will do it in action as we will do it before   5
     the Duke.

BOTTOM Peter Quince?

QUINCE What sayest thou, bully Bottom?

BOTTOM There are things in this comedy of Pyramus
     and Thisby that will never please. First, Pyramus   10
     must draw a sword to kill himself, which the ladies
     cannot abide. How answer you that?

SNOUT By'r lakin, a parlous fear.

STARVELING I believe we must leave the killing out,
     when all is done.   15

BOTTOM Not a whit! I have a device to make all well.
     Write me a prologue; and let the prologue seem to
     say we will do no harm with our swords, and that
     Pyramus is not killed indeed. And, for the more
     better assurance, tell them that I, Pyramus, am not   20
     Pyramus, but Bottom the weaver. This will put them
     out of fear.

QUINCE Well, we will have such a prologue, and it shall
     be written in eight and six.

BOTTOM No, make it two more, Let it be written in   25
     eight and eight.

SNOUT Will not the ladies be afeard of the lion?

STARVELING I fear it, I promise you.

138. Perforce: of necessity

157. prey: attack

161. of all loves: in the name of love

A MIDSUMMER NIGHT'S DREAM
Act 3. Scene 1

   0 Clowns: actors who play comic roles

   2. Pat: exactly as it should be; **marvels:** marvelously

   4. brake: thicket; **tiring-house:** dressing room

   8. bully: worthy

   13. By 'r lakin: "by our Lady"; **parlous:** perilous,
terrible

   24. eight and six: alternating eight- and six-syllable
lines

BOTTOM Masters, you ought to consider with yourself, to bring in (God shield us!) a lion among ladies, is a most dreadful thing. For there is not a more fearful wildfowl than your lion living, and we ought to look to 't. 30

SNOUT Therefore another prologue must tell he is not a lion. 35

BOTTOM Nay, you must name his name, and half his face must be seen through the lion's neck, and he himself must speak through, saying thus, or to the same defect: "Ladies" or "Fair ladies I would wish you," or "I would request you," or "I would entreat you not to fear, not to tremble! My life for yours. If you think I come hither as a lion, it were pity of my life. No I am no such thing; I am a man as other men are." And there indeed let him name his name and tell them plainly he is Snug the joiner. 40 45

QUINCE Well it shall be so. But there is two hard things: that is, to bring the moonlight into a chamber; for, you know, Pyramus and Thisby meet by moonlight.

SNOUT Doth the moon shine that night we play our play? 50

BOTTOM A calendar, a calendar! Look in the almanac. Find out moonshine, find out moonshine.

QUINCE *[takes out a book]* Yes, it doth shine that night.

BOTTOM Why, then may you leave a casement of the great chamber window, where we play, open, and the moon may shine in at the casement. 55

QUINCE Ay; or else one must come in with a bush of thorns and a lantern, and say he comes to disfigure or to present, the person of Moonshine. Then there is another thing: we must have a wall in the great chamber; for Pyramus and Thisby, says the story, did talk through the chink of a wall. 60

SNOUT You can never bring in a wall. What say you, Bottom? 65

BOTTOM Some man or other must present Wall. And let him have some plaster, or some loam, or some roughcast about him, to signify wall, or let him hold his fingers thus, and through that cranny shall Pyramus and Thisby whisper. 70

QUINCE If that may be, then all is well. Come, sit down, every mother's son, and rehearse your parts. Pyramus, you begin. When you have spoken your speech, enter into that brake, and so everyone according to his cue. 75

Enter Robin invisible to those onstage.

ROBIN *[aside]*
What hempen homespuns have we swagg'ring here
So near the cradle of the Fairy Queen?
What, a play toward? I'll be an auditor—
An actor too, perhaps, if I see cause.

QUINCE Speak, Pyramus. Thisby, stand forth. 80

BOTTOM *as Pyramus*
Thisby, the flowers of odious savors sweet,—

QUINCE Odors, odors!

BOTTOM *as Pyramus*
        —odors savors sweet:

39. defect: Bottom's error for "effect"

42-43. it were pity of my life: it would be risking my life

58-59. bush of thorns: In legend, in the moon there is a man who carries a bundle of sticks, a lantern, and has a dog.
59. disfigure: Quince's mistake for "figure" (represent)

77. cradle: the place where Titania is sleeping
78. toward: soon to be performed

So hath thy breath, my dearest Thisby dear.—
But hark, a voice! Stay thou but here awhile,   85
And by and by I will to thee appear
                    He exits.

ROBIN *[aside]*
A stranger Pyramus than e'er played here.
                    He exits.

FLUTE Must I speak now?

QUINCE Ay, marry, must you, for you must understand   **89. marry:** indeed
    he goes but to see a noise that he heard, and is to   90
    come again.

FLUTE *as Thisbe*
Most radiant Pyramus, most lily-white of hue,   *(Some of the comedy in the "Pyramus and Thisbe" scenes*
Of color like the red rose on triumphant brier,   *include poorly-crafted or forced rhymes, and truncated or*
Most brisky juvenal and eke most lovely Jew,   *extended words.)*
As true as truest horse, that yet would never tire,   95
I'll meet thee, Pyramus, at Ninny's tomb.

QUINCE 'Ninus' tomb,' man! Why, you must not   **97. Ninus' tomb:** In Ovid's *Metamorphoses*, the lovers
    speak that yet. That you answer to Pyramus. You   meet at the tomb of Ninus.
    speak all your part at once, cues and all.—
    Pyramus, enter. Your cue is past. It is, "never tire."   100

FLUTE O! *as Thisbe*
As true as truest horse, that yet would never tire.

        Enter Robin, and Bottom as Pyramus with the ass-head.   **103 with the ass-head:** wearing an "ass head"

BOTTOM *as Pyramus*
If I were fair, fair Thisby, I were only thine.

QUINCE O monstrous! O strange! We are haunted.
    Pray, masters, fly, masters! Help!   105
            Quince, Flute, Snout, Snug, and Starveling exit.

ROBIN
I'll follow you, I'll lead you about a round,
    Through bog, through bush, through brake,
        through brier:
Sometime a horse I'll be, sometime a hound,   110
    A hog, a headless bear, sometime a fire,
And neigh, and bark, and grunt, and roar, and burn,
    Like horse, hound, hog, bear, fire, at every turn.
                    Robin exits.

BOTTOM Why do they run away? This is a knavery of
    them to make me afeard.   115

                    Enter Snout.

SNOUT O Bottom, thou art changed! What do I see on
    thee?

BOTTOM What do you see? You see an ass-head of your
    own, do you?
                    Snout exits.
                    Enter Quince.

QUINCE Bless thee, Bottom! Bless thee! Thou art   120
    translated.
                    He exits.   **121. translated:** transformed

BOTTOM I see their knavery: this is to make an ass of me;
    to fright me, if they could. But I will not stir
    from this place, do what they can: I will walk up
    and down here, and I will sing, that they shall hear   125
    I am not afraid. *[He sings]*
The ouzel cock so black of hue,   **127. ouzel:** blackbird
With orange-tawny bill,
The throstle with his note so true,   **129. throstle:** thrush
The wren with little quill,—   130   **130. little quill:** a small, reedy voice

TITANIA *[waking up]*
What angel wakes me from my flowery bed?

BOTTOM [*sings*]
The finch, the sparrow and the lark,
The plainsong cuckoo gray,
Whose note full many a man doth mark,
And dares not answer nay;—   135
    for, indeed, who would set his wit to so foolish a
    bird? Who would give a bird the lie, though he cry
    "cuckoo" never so?

TITANIA
I pray thee, gentle mortal, sing again.
Mine ear is much enamored of thy note;   140
So is mine eye enthrallèd to thy shape;
And thy fair virtue's force perforce doth move me
On the first view to say, to swear, I love thee.

BOTTOM Methinks, mistress, you should have little
    reason for that. And yet, to say the truth, reason   145
    and love keep little company together nowadays.
    The more the pity that some honest neighbors will
    not make them friends. Nay, I can gleek upon
    occasion.

TITANIA
Thou art as wise as thou art beautiful.   150

BOTTOM Not so, neither: but if I had wit enough to get
    out of this wood, I have enough to serve mine own
    turn.

TITANIA
Out of this wood do not desire to go.
Thou shalt remain here, whether thou wilt or no.   155
I am a spirit of no common rate.
The summer still doth tend upon my state,
And I do love thee. Therefore, go with me.
I'll give thee fairies to attend on thee,
And they shall fetch thee jewels from the deep,   160
And sing while thou on pressèd flowers dost sleep.
And I will purge thy mortal grossness so
That thou shalt like an airy spirit go.—
Peaseblossom, Cobweb, Moth, and Mustardseed!

Enter four Fairies: Peaseblossom, Cobweb,
Mote, and Mustardseed.

PEASEBLOSSOM Ready.   165

COBWEB And I.

MOTE And I.

MUSTARDSEED And I.

ALL Where shall we go?

TITANIA
Be kind and courteous to this gentleman.   170
Hop in his walks and gambol in his eyes;
Feed him with apricocks and dewberries,
With purple grapes, green figs, and mulberries;
The honey-bags steal from the humble-bees,
And for night-tapers crop their waxen thighs   175
And light them at the fiery glowworm's eyes,
To have my love to bed and to arise;
And pluck the wings from painted butterflies
To fan the moonbeams from his sleeping eyes.
Nod to him, elves, and do him courtesies.   180

PEASEBLOSSOM Hail, mortal!

COBWEB Hail!

MOTE Hail!

MUSTARDSEED Hail!

---

136. who ... foolish: Proverbial: "Do not set your wit (use intelligence) against a fool's."
137. give...the lie: accuse...of lying
138. never so: as never before

140. note: song

142. perforce: whether I want to or not; **move me:** stir my passions

148. gleek: joke, jest

157. doth tend upon: serves; **state:** position of power

162. I will purge...grossness: Free you from mortality.

171. gambol: leap about

174. humble-bees: bumble bees

177. have: attend

BOTTOM I cry your worship's mercy, heartily—
I beseech your worship's name. `

COBWEB Cobweb.

BOTTOM I shall desire you of more acquaintance, good
Master Cobweb. If I cut my finger, I shall make
bold with you.—Your name, honest gentleman?

PEASEBLOSSOM Peaseblossom.

BOTTOM I pray you, commend me to Mistress Squash,
your mother, and to Master Peascod, your father.
Good Master Peaseblossom, I shall desire you of
more acquaintance too.—Your name, I beseech
you, sir?

MUSTARDSEED Mustardseed.

BOTTOM Good Master Mustardseed, I know your
patience well. That same cowardly, giantlike ox-beef
hath devoured many a gentleman of your house. I
promise you your kindred had made my eyes
water ere now. I desire you of more acquaintance,
good Master Mustardseed.

TITANIA
Come, wait upon him. Lead him to my bower.
 The moon, methinks, looks with a watery eye,
And when she weeps, weeps every little flower,
 Lamenting some enforcèd chastity.
Tie up my love's tongue bring him silently.
       They exit.

Act 3, Scene 2
    Enter Oberon, King of Fairies.

OBERON
I wonder if Titania be awaked;
Then, what it was that next came in her eye,
Which she must dote on in extremity.
    Enter Robin Goodfellow.
Here comes my messenger. How now, mad spirit?
What night-rule now about this haunted grove?

ROBIN
My mistress with a monster is in love.
Near to her close and consecrated bower,
While she was in her dull and sleeping hour,
A crew of patches, rude mechanicals,
That work for bread upon Athenian stalls,
Were met together to rehearse a play
Intended for great Theseus' nuptial day.
The shallowest thick-skin of that barren sort,
Who Pyramus presented, in their sport,
Forsook his scene and entered in a brake.
When I did him at this advantage take,
An ass's nole I fixèd on his head.
Anon his Thisbe must be answerèd,
And forth my mimic comes. When they him spy,
As wild geese that the creeping fowler eye,
Or russet-pated choughs, many in sort,
Rising and cawing at the gun's report,
Sever themselves and madly sweep the sky,
So, at his sight, away his fellows fly;
And, at our stamp, here o'er and o'er one falls.
He murder cries and help from Athens calls.
Their sense thus weak, lost with their fears thus
 strong,
Made senseless things begin to do them wrong;
For briers and thorns at their apparel snatch,
Some sleeves, some hats, from yielders all things
 catch.

185

190

195

200

205

5

10

15

20

25

30

A MIDSUMMER NIGHT'S DREAM
Act 3. Scene 2

3. in extremity: completely, excessively

5. night-rule: disorder, odd goings-on; **haunted:** much visited
7. close: secret

9. patches: simpletons; **rude:** unrefined; **mechanicals:** craftsmen

13. barren: boring
14. sport: theatrical endeavor
15. Foresook: exited; **brake:** thicket

17. nole: head
18. Anon: soon
19. mimic: comedian
20. fowler: bird hunter
21. russet-pated ... sort: large flock of birds with brownish heads
23. Sever themselves: split up

25. at our stamp: over our stumps or tree trunks

31-32. from ... catch: it is easy to snatch at cowards.

I led them on in this distracted fear,
And left sweet Pyramus translated there.
When in that moment, so it came to pass,   35
Titania waked and straightway loved an ass.

OBERON
This falls out better than I could devise.
But hast thou yet latched the Athenian's eyes
With the love juice, as I did bid thee do?

ROBIN
I took him sleeping,—that is finished too,—   40
And the Athenian woman by his side,
That, when he waked, of force she must be eyed.

                    Enter Demetrius and Hermia.

OBERON
Stand close. This is the same Athenian.

ROBIN
This is the woman, but not this the man.
                    They step aside.

DEMETRIUS
O, why rebuke you him that loves you so?   45
Lay breath so bitter on your bitter foe!

HERMIA
Now I but chide, but I should use thee worse,
For thou, I fear, hast given me cause to curse.
If thou hast slain Lysander in his sleep,
Being o'er shoes in blood, plunge in the deep   50
And kill me too.
The sun was not so true unto the day
As he to me. Would he have stolen away
From sleeping Hermia? I'll believe as soon
This whole earth may be bored, and that the moon   55
May through the centre creep and so displease
Her brother's noontide with th' Antipodes.
It cannot be but thou hast murdered him.
So should a murderer look, so dead, so grim.

DEMETRIUS
So should the murdered look, and so should I,   60
Pierced through the heart with your stern cruelty.
Yet you, the murderer, look as bright, as clear,
As yonder Venus in her glimmering sphere.

HERMIA
What's this to my Lysander? Where is he?
Ah, good Demetrius, wilt thou give him me?   65

DEMETRIUS
I had rather give his carcass to my hounds.

HERMIA
Out, dog! Out, cur! Thou driv'st me past the bounds
Of maiden's patience. Hast thou slain him, then?
Henceforth be never numbered among men.
O, once tell true! Tell true, even for my sake!   70
Durst thou have looked upon him being awake,
And hast thou killed him sleeping? O brave touch!
Could not a worm, an adder, do so much?
An adder did it, for with doubler tongue
Than thine, thou serpent, never adder stung.   75

DEMETRIUS
You spend your passion on a misprised mood.
I am not guilty of Lysander's blood,
Nor is he dead, for aught that I can tell.

HERMIA
I pray thee, tell me then that he is well.

34. translated: transformed

37. falls out: occurs
38. latched: captured

42. of force: of necessity, inevitably

43. Stand close: an order to hide

50. o'er shoes: ankle-deep

55. bored: drilled through
56. displease: create chaos
57. her brother: the sun (the moon's brother);
Antipodes: (switching to) the opposite side of the globe

73. worm: snake

76. misprised: mistaken

DEMETRIUS
And if I could, what should I get therefor?   80

HERMIA
A privilege never to see me more.
And from thy hated presence part I so.
See me no more, whether he be dead or no.
                              She exits.

DEMETRIUS
There is no following her in this fierce vein.
Here therefore for a while I will remain.   85
So sorrow's heaviness doth heavier grow
For debt that bankrupt sleep doth sorrow owe,
Which now in some slight measure it will pay,
If for his tender here I make some stay.
                    He lies down and falls asleep.

OBERON *[to Robin]*
What hast thou done? Thou hast mistaken quite   90
And laid the love juice on some true-love's sight.
Of thy misprision must perforce ensue
Some true-love turned and not a false turned true.

ROBIN
Then fate o'errules, that, one man holding troth,
A million fail, confounding oath on oath.   95

OBERON
About the wood go swifter than the wind,
And Helena of Athens look thou find.
All fancy-sick she is and pale of cheer
With sighs of love, that costs the fresh blood dear.
By some illusion see thou bring her here.   100
I'll charm his eyes against she do appear.

ROBIN
I go, I go, look how I go,
Swifter than arrow from the Tartar's bow.
                              He exits.

OBERON *[applying the nectar to Demetrius' eyes.]*
  Flower of this purple dye,
  Hit with Cupid's archery,   105
  Sink in apple of his eye.
  When his love he doth espy,
  Let her shine as gloriously
  As the Venus of the sky.
  When thou wak'st, if she be by,   110
  Beg of her for remedy.
                    Enter Robin.

ROBIN
  Captain of our fairy band,
  Helena is here at hand,
  And the youth, mistook by me,
  Pleading for a lover's fee.   115
  Shall we their fond pageant see?
  Lord, what fools these mortals be!
OBERON
  Stand aside. The noise they make
  Will cause Demetrius to awake.

ROBIN
  Then will two at once woo one.   120
  That must needs be sport alone;
  And those things do best please me
  That befall prepost'rously.
                    Enter Lysander and Helena.

LYSANDER
Why should you think that I should woo in scorn?
  Scorn and derision never come in tears.   125

92. Of thy misprision: because of your mistake; **must perforce ensue:** it must therefore follow

94. fate o'errules: fate has decided; **holding troth:** keeping his oath; **confounding:** destroying

98. cheer: face
99. costs ... dear: Sighs were thought to weaken blood.

101. against: in preparation for the time

114. the youth: Lysander
115. fee: reward
116. fond pageant: foolish exhibition

121. sport alone: unparalleled entertainment

Look, when I vow, I weep; and vows so born,
  In their nativity all truth appears.
How can these things in me seem scorn to you,
Bearing the badge of faith, to prove them true?

HELENA
You do advance your cunning more and more.   130
  When truth kills truth, O devilish-holy fray!
These vows are Hermia's. Will you give her o'er?
  Weigh oath with oath, and you will nothing
      weigh:
Your vows to her and me, put in two scales,   135
Will even weigh, and both as light as tales.

LYSANDER
I had no judgment when to her I swore.

HELENA
Nor none, in my mind, now you give her o'er.

LYSANDER
Demetrius loves her, and he loves not you.

DEMETRIUS *[waking up]*
O Helena, goddess, nymph, perfect, divine!   140
To what, my love, shall I compare thine eyne?
Crystal is muddy. O, how ripe in show
Thy lips, those kissing cherries, tempting grow!
That pure congealèd white, high Taurus snow,
Fanned with the eastern wind, turns to a crow   145
When thou hold'st up thy hand. O, let me kiss
This princess of pure white, this seal of bliss!

HELENA
O spite! O hell! I see you all are bent
To set against me for your merriment.
If you were civil and knew courtesy,   150
You would not do me thus much injury.
Can you not hate me, as I know you do,
But you must join in souls to mock me too?
If you were men, as men you are in show,
You would not use a gentle lady so,   155
To vow and swear and superpraise my parts,
When, I am sure, you hate me with your hearts.
You both are rivals, and love Hermia,
And now both rivals, to mock Helena.
A trim exploit, a manly enterprise,   160
To conjure tears up in a poor maid's eyes
With your derision! None of noble sort
Would so offend a virgin and extort
A poor soul's patience, all to make you sport.

LYSANDER
You are unkind, Demetrius. Be not so,   165
For you love Hermia; this you know I know:
And here, with all goodwill, with all my heart,
In Hermia's love I yield you up my part.
And yours of Helena to me bequeath,
Whom I do love and will do till my death.   170

HELENA
Never did mockers waste more idle breath.

DEMETRIUS
Lysander, keep thy Hermia; I will none.
If e'er I loved her, all that love is gone.
My heart to her but as guest-wise sojourned,
And now to Helen is it home returned,   175
There to remain.

  LYSANDER   Helen, it is not so.

DEMETRIUS
Disparage not the faith thou dost not know,

---

129. badge of faith: his tears

130. advance: reveal, show off
131. truth kills truth: Lysander's current vow to Helena negates his past vow to Hermia; **devilish-holy fray:** a battle of contradictions
132. give her o'er: toss her aside

141. eyne: eyes

144. Taurus: a mountain range in Asia

147. princess of pure white: her hand; **seal:** guarantee, vow

153. join in souls: unite as one, conspire

160. trim: fit (said sarcastically)

163. extort: take forcibly

172. I will none: I want none of her

174. sojourned: stay with, visited

Lest, to thy peril, thou aby it dear.
Look, where thy love comes. Yonder is thy dear.　　　180
Enter Hermia.

HERMIA *[to Lysander]*
Dark night, that from the eye his function takes,
The ear more quick of apprehension makes;
Wherein it doth impair the seeing sense,
It pays the hearing double recompense.
Thou art not by mine eye, Lysander, found;　　　185
Mine ear, I thank it, brought me to thy sound.
But why unkindly didst thou leave me so?

LYSANDER
Why should he stay, whom love doth press to go?

HERMIA
What love could press Lysander from my side?

LYSANDER
Lysander's love, that would not let him bide,　　　190
Fair Helena, who more engilds the night
Than all you fiery oes and eyes of light.
Why seek'st thou me? Could not this make thee
　　know,
The hate I bear thee made me leave thee so?　　　195

HERMIA
You speak not as you think. It cannot be.

HELENA
Lo, she is one of this confederacy!
Now I perceive they have conjoin'd all three
To fashion this false sport, in spite of me.—
Injurious Hermia, most ungrateful maid,　　　200
Have you conspired, have you with these contrived,
To bait me with this foul derision?
Is all the counsel that we two have shared,
The sisters' vows, the hours that we have spent
When we have chid the hasty-footed time　　　205
For parting us,—O, is it all forgot?
All schooldays' friendship, childhood innocence?
We, Hermia, like two artificial gods,
Have with our needles created both one flower,
Both on one sampler, sitting on one cushion,　　　210
Both warbling of one song, both in one key,
As if our hands, our sides, voices and minds
Had been incorporate. So we grow together
Like to a double cherry, seeming parted,
But yet an union in partition;　　　215
Two lovely berries moulded on one stem;
So, with two seeming bodies, but one heart,
Two of the first, like coats in heraldry,
Due but to one and crownèd with one crest.
And will you rent our ancient love asunder,　　　220
To join with men in scorning your poor friend?
It is not friendly, 'tis not maidenly.
Our sex, as well as I, may chide you for it,
Though I alone do feel the injury.

HERMIA
I am amazed at your passionate words.　　　225
I scorn you not: it seems that you scorn me.

HELENA
Have you not set Lysander, as in scorn,
To follow me and praise my eyes and face,
And made your other love, Demetrius,
Who even but now did spurn me with his foot,　　　230
To call me goddess, nymph, divine and rare,
Precious, celestial? Wherefore speaks he this
To her he hates? And wherefore doth Lysander

179. aby it dear: pay a great cost for it

183. Wherein: while

188. press: urge

192. oes: circles of light, spangles

199. In spite of: to spite

202. bait: ridicule

205. chid: scolded

208. artificial: handy, crafty

213. incorporate: combined in one body

218-19. Two of the first... crest: Like the heraldic crests of two families that are combined into one crest to symbolize their union
220. rent: tear

223. Our sex: all of our gender

230. spurn: kick

232. Wherefore: why

Deny your love (so rich within his soul)
And tender me, forsooth, affection,   235
But by your setting on, by your consent?
What thought I be not so in grace as you,
So hung upon with love, so fortunate,
But miserable most, to love unloved?
This you should pity rather than despise.   240

HERMIA
I understand not what you mean by this.

HELENA
Ay, do. Persever, counterfeit sad looks,
Make mouths upon me when I turn my back.
Wink each at other, hold the sweet jest up.
This sport, well carried, shall be chronicled.   245
If you have any pity, grace, or manners,
You would not make me such an argument.
But fare ye well - Tis partly my own fault,
Which death or absence soon shall remedy.

LYSANDER
Stay, gentle Helena. Hear my excuse,   250
My love, my life, my soul, fair Helena.

HELENA
O excellent!

HERMIA *[to Lysander]*
Sweet, do not scorn her so.

DEMETRIUS *[to Lysander]*
If she cannot entreat, I can compel.

LYSANDER
Thou canst compel no more than she entreat.   255
Thy threats have no more strength than her weak
   prayers.—
Helen, I love thee; by my life, I do.
I swear by that which I will lose for thee,
To prove him false that says I love thee not.   260

DEMETRIUS
I say I love thee more than he can do.

LYSANDER
If thou say so, withdraw, and prove it too.

DEMETRIUS
Quick, come!

HERMIA
         Lysander, whereto tends all this?
                  She takes hold of Lysander.

LYSANDER
Away, you Ethiop!   265

DEMETRIUS *[to Hermia]* No, no. He'll
Seem to break loose. *[To Lysander]* Take on as you
   would follow,
But yet come not. You are a tame man, go!

LYSANDER *[to Hermia]*
Hang off, thou cat, thou burr! Vile thing, let loose,   270
Or I will shake thee from me like a serpent!

HERMIA
Why are you grown so rude? What change is this?
Sweet love?

LYSANDER   Thy love! Out, tawny Tartar, out!
Out, loathèd med'cine! O hated potion, hence!   275

HERMIA
Do you not jest?

---

235. tender: give; **forsooth:** in truth
236. setting on: beginning it
237. in grace: popular

242. Persever: persevere; **sad:** serious
243. mouths upon: faces at

245. carried: handled; **chronicled:** recorded in history

247. argument: example

254. she: Hermia; **entreat:** convince

259. by that: by my life

262. withdraw, and prove it: Lysander challenges Demetrius to prove his love for Helena in a duel.

265. Ethiop: perhaps a reference to Hermia's dark hair or complexion.
266-68. No ... follow: *(These lines are disputed with different versions appearing in the earliest editions.)*
267. seem: pretend; **take on as:** act as if

274. Tartar: Gypsy (another reference to Hermia's coloring)

HELENA   Yes, sooth, and so do you.

LYSANDER
Demetrius, I will keep my word with thee.

DEMETRIUS
I would I had your bond, for I perceive
A weak bond holds you: I'll not trust your word.   280

LYSANDER
What, should I hurt her, strike her, kill her dead?
Although I hate her, I'll not harm her so.

HERMIA
What, can you do me greater harm than hate?
Hate me! Wherefore? O me, what news, my love?
Am not I Hermia? Are not you Lysander?   285
I am as fair now as I was erewhile.
Since night you loved me; yet since night you left
     me.
Why, then you left me—O, the gods forbid!—
In earnest, shall I say?   290

LYSANDER   Ay, by my life,
And never did desire to see thee more.
Therefore be out of hope, of question, of doubt.
Be certain, nothing truer; 'tis no jest
That I do hate thee and love Helena.   295
               Hermia turns him loose.

HERMIA
O me! *[To Helena]* You juggler, you canker blossom!
You thief of love! What, have you come by night
And stol'n my love's heart from him?

HELENA
                    Fine, i' faith!
Have you no modesty, no maiden shame,   300
No touch of bashfulness? What, will you tear
Impatient answers from my gentle tongue?
Fie, fie, you counterfeit, you puppet, you!

HERMIA
"Puppet"? Why so? Ay, that way goes the game.
Now I perceive that she hath made compare   305
Between our statures; she hath urged her height,
And with her personage, her tall personage,
Her height, forsooth, she hath prevailed with him.
And are you grown so high in his esteem
Because I am so dwarfish and so low?   310
How low am I, thou painted maypole? Speak!
How low am I? I am not yet so low
But that my nails can reach unto thine eyes.

HELENA
I pray you, though you mock me, gentlemen,
Let her not hurt me: I was never curst;   315
I have no gift at all in shrewishness.
I am a right maid for my cowardice.
Let her not strike me. You perhaps may think,
Because she is something lower than myself,
That I can match her.   320

HERMIA   "Lower?" Hark, again!

HELENA
Good Hermia, do not be so bitter with me.
I evermore did love you, Hermia,
Did ever keep your counsels, never wronged you—
Save that, in love unto Demetrius,   325
I told him of your stealth unto this wood.
He followed you; for love, I followed him.
But he hath chid me hence and threatened me
To strike me, spurn me, nay, to kill me too.

277. sooth: truly

278. my word with thee: I will fight you.

279. bond: legal binding contract
280. weak bond: this refers to Hermia, who is holding back Lysander.

286. erewhile: a little while earlier

296. juggler: trickster, deceiver; **canker blossom:** a worm that destroys flower buds

306. urged: proposed

315. curst: mean
316. shrewishness: meanness
317. a right maid: a true girl indeed

328. chid me hence: scolded me in an effort to force me away

And now, so you will let me quiet go,   330
To Athens will I bear my folly back
And follow you no further. Let me go.
You see how simple and how fond I am.

HERMIA
Why, get you gone. Who is 't that hinders you?

HELENA
A foolish heart, that I leave here behind.   335

HERMIA
What, with Lysander?

HELENA   With Demetrius.

LYSANDER
Be not afraid; she shall not harm thee, Helena.

DEMETRIUS
No, sir, she shall not, though you take her part.

HELENA
O, when she's angry, she is keen and shrewd.   340
She was a vixen when she went to school,
And though she be but little, she is fierce.

HERMIA
"Little" again! Nothing but "low" and "little"?
Why will you suffer her to flout me thus?
Let me come to her.   345

LYSANDER   Get you gone, you dwarf,
You minimus, of hind'ring knotgrass made,
You bead, you acorn—

DEMETRIUS   You are too officious
In her behalf that scorns your services.   350
Let her alone. Speak not of Helena.
Take not her part. For, if thou dost intend
Never so little show of love to her,
Thou shalt aby it.

LYSANDER   Now she holds me not.   355
Now follow, if thou dar'st, to try whose right,
Of thine or mine, is most in Helena.

DEMETRIUS
"Follow?" Nay, I'll go with thee, cheek by jowl.
Demetrius and Lysander exit.

HERMIA
You, mistress, all this coil is long of you.
Helena retreats.
Nay, go not back.

HELENA   I will not trust you, I,
Nor longer stay in your curst company.
Your hands than mine are quicker for a fray.
My legs are longer though, to run away.
She exits.

HERMIA
I am amazed, and know not what to say.   365
She exits.

OBERON *[to Robin]*
This is thy negligence. Still thou mistak'st,
Or else committ'st thy knaveries wilfully.

ROBIN
Believe me, king of shadows, I mistook.
Did not you tell me I should know the man
By the Athenian garment he had on?   370
And so far blameless proves my enterprise
That I have 'nointed an Athenian's eyes;
And so far am I glad it so did sort,
As this their jangling I esteem a sport.

330. so: if

333. fond: foolish

340. keen: sharply cruel; **shrewd:** mean

344. suffer: allow
345. come to her: attack her

347. minimus: tiniest of beings; **knotgrass:** a weed that supposedly stunted growth

354. aby: pay for

359. coil: trouble; **long:** because

373. so did sort: happened this way

OBERON

Thou seest these lovers seek a place to fight.   375

Hie, therefore, Robin, overcast the night;

The starry welkin cover thou anon

With drooping fog as black as Acheron,

And lead these testy rivals so astray

As one come not within another's way.   380

Like to Lysander sometime frame thy tongue;

Then stir Demetrius up with bitter wrong.

And sometime rail thou like Demetrius.

And from each other look thou lead them thus,

Till o'er their brows death-counterfeiting sleep   385

With leaden legs and batty wings doth creep.

Then crush this herb into Lysander's eye,

He gives the flower to Robin.

Whose liquor hath this virtuous property,

To take from thence all error with his might

And make his eyeballs roll with wonted sight.   390

When they next wake, all this derision

Shall seem a dream and fruitless vision.

And back to Athens shall the lovers wend,

With league whose date till death shall never end.

Whiles I in this affair do thee employ,   395

I'll to my queen and beg her Indian boy;

And then I will her charmed eye release

From monster's view, and all things shall be peace.

ROBIN

My fairy lord, this must be done with haste,

For night's swift dragons cut the clouds full fast,   400

And yonder shines Aurora's harbinger,

At whose approach, ghosts, wand'ring here and
    there,

Troop home to churchyards. Damnèd spirits all,

That in crossways and floods have burial,   405

Already to their wormy beds are gone.

For fear lest day should look their shames upon,

They willfully themselves exile from light

And must for aye consort with black-browed night.

OBERON

But we are spirits of another sort.   410

I with the Morning's love have oft made sport

And, like a forester, the groves may tread

Even till the eastern gate, all fiery-red,

Opening on Neptune with fair blessèd beams,

Turns into yellow gold his salt-green streams.   415

But notwithstanding, haste! Make no delay.

We may effect this business yet ere day.

He exits.

ROBIN

  Up and down, up and down,

  I will lead them up and down.

  I am feared in field and town.   420

  Goblin, lead them up and down.

Here comes one.

Enter Lysander.

LYSANDER

Where art thou, proud Demetrius? Speak thou now.

ROBIN *[in Demetrius' voice]*

Here, villain, drawn and ready. Where art thou?

LYSANDER I will be with thee straight.   425

ROBIN *[in Demetrius' voice]*   Follow me, then,

to plainer ground.

Lysander exits. Enter Demetrius.

---

376. Hie: hurry

377. welkin: sky; **anon:** as soon as possible

378. Acheron: hell, a river in Hades

380. As one come: so that one comes

387. herb: plant, flower

388. liquor: juice

389. his might: the herb's strength

390. wonted sight: normal vision

394. With league ... end: united in an oath that's
duration is until death

401. Aurora: the dawn; **harbinger:** person or thing
that announces

405. That in crossways ... burial: that were not
buried in sacred ground; **crossways:** crossroads, where
suicides were buried

411. I with...made sport: I can play in the morning
sun, or I have often made love to Cephalus, the goddess of
the morning.
  413. the eastern gate: where the sun rises
  414. Neptune: the ocean

421. Goblin: hobgoblin (another name for Robin
Goodfellow)

424. drawn: with my sword out of its sheath
425. straight: immediately

427. plainer: flatter

DEMETRIUS   Lysander, speak again.
Thou runaway, thou coward, art thou fled?
Speak! In some bush? Where dost thou hide thy head?   430

ROBIN *[in Lysander's voice]*
Thou coward, art thou bragging to the stars,
Telling the bushes that thou look'st for wars,
And wilt not come? Come, recreant; come, thou
     child!   435
I'll whip thee with a rod. He is defiled
That draws a sword on thee.

DEMETRIUS   Yea, art thou there?

ROBIN *[in Lysander's voice]*
Follow my voice. We'll try no manhood here.
            They exit. Enter Lysander.

LYSANDER
He goes before me and still dares me on.   440
When I come where he calls, then he is gone.
The villain is much lighter-heeled than I.
I followed fast, but faster he did fly,
That fallen am I in dark uneven way,
And here will rest me. Come, thou gentle day,   445
For if but once thou show me thy gray light,
I'll find Demetrius and revenge this spite.
            He lies down and sleeps.
            Enter Robin and Demetrius.

ROBIN *[in Lysander's voice]*
Ho, ho, ho! Coward, why com'st thou not?

DEMETRIUS
Abide me, if thou dar'st, for well I wot
Thou runn'st before me, shifting every place,   450
And dar'st not stand, nor look me in the face.
Where art thou now?

ROBIN *[in Lysander's voice]* Come hither. I am here.

DEMETRIUS
Nay, then, thou mock'st me. Thou shalt buy this
     dear   455
If ever I thy face by daylight see.
Now, go thy way. Faintness constraineth me
To measure out my length on this cold bed.
By day's approach look to be visited.
            He lies down and sleeps..
            Enter Helena

HELENA
O weary night, O long and tedious night,   460
  Abate thy hour! Shine comforts from the east,
That I may back to Athens by daylight
  From these that my poor company detest.
And sleep, that sometimes shuts up sorrow's eye,
Steal me awhile from mine own company.
            She lies down and sleeps.

ROBIN
  Yet but three? Come one more.
  Two of both kinds make up four.
  Here she comes, curst and sad:
  Cupid is a knavish lad
  Thus to make poor females mad.   470

            Enter Hermia.
HERMIA
Never so weary, never so in woe,
Bedabbled with the dew and torn with briers,
I can no further crawl, no further go.
My legs can keep no pace with my desires.

434. recreant: coward

439. try no manhood: have no test of our courage

449. Abide me: wait for me; **wot:** know

454-55. buy this dear: pay dearly for this

461. Abate: shorten

468. curst: angry

Here will I rest me till the break of day.   475
Heavens shield Lysander, if they mean a fray!
                          She lies down and sleeps.

ROBIN
 On the ground
 Sleep sound:
 I'll apply
 To your eye,   480
 Gentle lover, remedy.
                    Robin applies the nectar to Lysander's eyes.
 When thou wak'st,
 Thou tak'st
 True delight
 In the sight   485
Of thy former lady's eye.
And the country proverb known,
That every man should take his own,
In your waking shall be shown.
 Jack shall have Jill;   490
 Naught shall go ill;
The man shall have his mare again, and all shall be well.
                          He exits.

Act 4, Scene 1
      Lysander, Demetrius, Helena, and Hermia lying asleep.
      Enter Titania, Queen of Fairies, and Bottom and Fairies
      and Oberon, the King, behind them unseen by those onstage.

TITANIA
Come, sit thee down upon this flowery bed,
 While I thy amiable cheeks do coy,
And stick musk-roses in thy sleek smooth head,
 And kiss thy fair large ears, my gentle joy.

BOTTOM Where's Peaseblossom?   5

PEASEBLOSSOM Ready.

BOTTOM Scratch my head Peaseblossom. Where's
 Monsieur Cobweb?

COBWEB Ready.

BOTTOM Monsieur Cobweb, good monsieur, get you   10
 your weapons in your hand, and kill me a red-hipped
 humble-bee on the top of a thistle, and, good
 monsieur, bring me the honey-bag. Do not fret
 yourself too much in the action, monsieur, and,
 good monsieur, have a care the honey-bag break   15
 not; I would be loath to have you overflown with a
 honey-bag, signior. *[Cobweb exits]* Where's Monsieur
 Mustardseed?

MUSTARDSEED Ready.

BOTTOM Give me your neaf, Monsieur Mustardseed.   20
 Pray you, leave your courtesy, good monsieur.

MUSTARDSEED What's your Will?

BOTTOM Nothing, good monsieur, but to help
 Cavalery Cobweb to scratch. I must to the barber's,
 monsieur; for methinks I am marvellous hairy about   25
 the face. And I am such a tender ass, if my hair do
 but tickle me, I must scratch.

TITANIA
What, wilt thou hear some music, my sweet love?

BOTTOM I have a reasonable good ear in music. Let's
 have the tongs and the bones.   30

---

476. mean: intend to; **fray:** fight

A MIDSUMMER NIGHT'S DREAM
Act 4. Scene 1

2. coy: caress

16. overflown with: covered in

20. neaf: fist, hand

24. Cavalery: Cavalier

30. the tongs and the bones: primitive musical
instruments used in rustic music

TITANIA
Or say, sweet love, what thou desirest to eat.

BOTTOM Truly, a peck of provender: I could munch
  your good dry oats. Methinks I have a great desire
  to a bottle of hay: good hay, sweet hay, hath no
  fellow.   35

32. provender: hay

34. bottle: bundle
35. fellow: equal

TITANIA
I have a venturous fairy that shall seek
The squirrel's hoard, and fetch thee new nuts.

BOTTOM I had rather have a handful or two of dried
  peas. But, I pray you, let none of your people stir
  me; I have an exposition of sleep come upon me.   40

40. exposition of: Bottom's error for "disposition to"

TITANIA
Sleep thou, and I will wind thee in my arms.—
Fairies, begone, and be all ways away.
                              Fairies exit.
So doth the woodbine the sweet honeysuckle
Gently entwist; the female ivy so
Enrings the barky fingers of the elm.   45
O, how I love thee! How I dote on thee!
                    Bottom and Titania sleep.
                    Enter Robin Goodfellow.

OBERON
Welcome, good Robin. Seest thou this sweet sight?
Her dotage now I do begin to pity.

48. dotage: infatuation

For, meeting her of late behind the wood,
Seeking sweet favors from this hateful fool,   50
I did upbraid her and fall out with her.
For she his hairy temples then had rounded
With a coronet of fresh and fragrant flowers;
And that same dew, which sometime on the buds

54. sometime: formerly

Was wont to swell like round and orient pearls,   55
Stood now within the pretty flouriets' eyes
Like tears that did their own disgrace bewail.

55. orient: radiant, lustrous
56. flouriets: little flowers

When I had at my pleasure taunted her
And she in mild terms begged my patience,
I then did ask of her her changeling child,   60
Which straight she gave me, and her fairy sent

61. straight: at once

To bear him to my bower in Fairyland.
And now I have the boy, I will undo
This hateful imperfection of her eyes.

64. hateful...her eyes: evil vision-altering spell

And, gentle Puck, take this transformed scalp   65
From off the head of this Athenian swain,
That, he awaking when the other do,
May all to Athens back again repair
And think no more of this night's accidents

67. other: others
68. repair: travel
69. accidents: unfortunate events

But as the fierce vexation of a dream.   70
But first I will release the Fairy Queen.
              He applies the nectar to her eyes.

72. wast wont to: used to

  Be as thou wast wont to be.
  See as thou wast wont to see.
  Dian's bud o'er Cupid's flower
  Hath such force and blessèd power.   75
Now, my Titania, wake you, my sweet queen.

TITANIA *(waking)*
My Oberon, what visions have I seen!
Methought I was enamored of an ass.

OBERON
There lies your love.

TITANIA   How came these things to pass?   80
O, how mine eyes do loathe his visage now!

81. visage: face

OBERON
Silence awhile.—Robin, take off this head.—

Titania, music call; and strike more dead
Than common sleep of all these five the sense.

TITANIA
Music, ho, music, such as charmeth sleep!   85

ROBIN [*removing the ass-head from Bottom*]
Now, when thou wak'st, with thine own fool's eyes
  peep.
OBERON
Sound, music! [*Music*]
           Come, my queen, take hands with me,
And rock the ground whereon these sleepers be.   90
           Titania and Oberon dance.
Now thou and I are new in amity,
And will tomorrow midnight solemnly
Dance in Duke Theseus' house triumphantly,
And bless it to all fair prosperity.
There shall the pairs of faithful lovers be   95
Wedded, with Theseus, all in jollity.

ROBIN
  Fairy king, attend, and mark.
  I do hear the morning lark.

OBERON
  Then, my queen, in silence sad
  Trip we after the night's shade.   100
  We the globe can compass soon,
  Swifter than the wand'ring moon.

TITANIA
  Come, my lord, and in our flight
  Tell me how it came this night
  That I sleeping here was found   105
  With these mortals on the ground.
           Oberon, Titania and Robin exit.
           Wind horn.
           Enter THESEUS, HIPPOLYTA, EGEUS, and train.

THESEUS
Go, one of you, find out the Forester.
For now our observation is performed;
And since we have the vaward of the day,
My love shall hear the music of my hounds.   110
Uncouple in the western valley; let them go.
Dispatch, I say, and find the Forester.
           A Servant exits.
We will, fair queen, up to the mountain's top
And mark the musical confusion
Of hounds and echo in conjunction.   115

HIPPOLYTA
I was with Hercules and Cadmus once,
When in a wood of Crete they bayed the bear
With hounds of Sparta. Never did I hear
Such gallant chiding, for, besides the groves,
The skies, the fountains, every region near   120
Seemed all one mutual cry. I never heard
So musical a discord, such sweet thunder.

THESEUS
My hounds are bred out of the Spartan kind,
So flewed, so sanded, and their heads are hung
With ears that sweep away the morning dew;   125
Crook-kneed, and dewlapped like Thessalian bulls;
Slow in pursuit, but matched in mouth like bells,
Each under each. A cry more tunable
Was never holloed to, nor cheered with horn,
In Crete, in Sparta, nor in Thessaly.   130
Judge when you hear.—But, soft! What nymphs are
  these?

84. these five: Bottom and the four lovers

92. solemnly: ceremoniously
93. triumphantly: magnificently

99. sad: grave

108. our observation: our observance of May Day
109. since ... day: since it is still early **vaward:** the beginning part of a vanguard
111. Uncouple: unleash the hounds

116. Cadmus: legendary founder of the city of Thebes
117. bayed: brought to bay

119. chiding: barking

124. So: like those of Sparta; **flewed:** with large folds of flesh about the mouth; **sanded:** sand colored
126. dewlapped: with folds of skin under their necks
127-28. matched ... bells: their cry was like a set of bells; **Each under each:** like notes on a scale
128. cry: pack; **tunable:** tuneful

131. soft: hold on

EGEUS
My lord, this is my daughter here asleep,
And this, Lysander; this Demetrius is;
This Helena, old Nedar's Helena: 135
I wonder of their being here together.

THESEUS
No doubt they rose up early to observe
The rite of May, and hearing our intent,
Came here in grace our solemnity.   **139. grace:** honor, **solemnity:** observance
But speak, Egeus. Is not this the day   140
That Hermia should give answer of her choice?

EGEUS
It is, my lord.
THESEUS
Go, bid the huntsmen wake them with their horns.
                    A Servant exits.
               Shout within. Wind horns.

    Lysander, Demetrius, Helena, and Hermia wake and start up.
Good morrow, friends. Saint Valentine is past:
Begin these wood-birds but to couple now?   145

         Demetrius, Helena, Hermia and Lysander kneel.

LYSANDER
Pardon, my lord.

THESEUS   I pray you all, stand up.
                         They rise.
I know you two are rival enemies.
How comes this gentle concord in the world,
That hatred is so far from jealousy   150   **150. jealousy:** suspicion
To sleep by hate and fear no enmity?

LYSANDER
My lord, I shall reply amazèdly,
Half sleep, half waking. But as yet, I swear,
I cannot truly say how I came here.
But, as I think,—for truly would I speak,   155
And now do I bethink me, so it is:
I came with Hermia hither. Our intent
Was to be gone from Athens, where we might,
Without the peril of the Athenian law.—

EGEUS
Enough, enough.—My lord; you have enough.   160
I beg the law, the law, upon his head.
They would have stol'n away.—They would,
  Demetrius,
Thereby to have defeated you and me:
You of your wife and me of my consent,   165
Of my consent that she should be your wife.

DEMETRIUS
My lord, fair Helen told me of their stealth,
Of this their purpose hither to this wood,
And I in fury hither followed them,
Fair Helena in fancy following me.   170   **170. in fancy:** due to her love
But, my good lord, I wot not by what power   **171. wot:** know
(But by some power it is) my love to Hermia,
Melted as the snow, seems to me now
As the remembrance of an idle gaud   **174. idle gaud:** worthless trinket
Which in my childhood I did dote upon,   175
And all the faith, the virtue of my heart,   **176. virtue:** power
The object and the pleasure of mine eye,
Is only Helena. To her, my lord,
Was I betrothed ere I saw Hermia.
But, like a sickness, did I loathe this food.   180
But, as in health, come to my natural taste,
Now I do wish it, love it, long for it,
And will for evermore be true to it.

THESEUS
Fair lovers, you are fortunately met.
Of this discourse we more will hear anon.—   185
Egeus, I will overbear your will,
For in the temple by and by, with us,
These couples shall eternally be knit.—
And, for the morning now is something worn,
Our purposed hunting shall be set aside.   190
Away with us to Athens. Three and three,
We'll hold a feast in great solemnity.
Come, Hippolyta.
                Theseus, Hippolyta, Egeus, and train exit

DEMETRIUS
These things seem small and undistinguishable,
Like far-off mountains turnèd into clouds.   195

HERMIA
Methinks I see these things with parted eye,
When every thing seems double.

HELENA   So methinks.
And I have found Demetrius like a jewel,
Mine own and not mine own.   200

DEMETRIUS   Are you sure
That we are awake? It seems to me
That yet we sleep, we dream. Do not you think
The duke was here, and bid us follow him?

HERMIA
Yea, and my father.   205

HELENA   And Hippolyta.

LYSANDER
And he did bid us follow to the temple.

DEMETRIUS
Why, then, we are awake. Let's follow him
And by the way let us recount our dreams.

                                    Lovers exit.

BOTTOM *[Waking Up]* When my cue comes, call me,
   and I will answer. My next is, "Most fair Pyramus."
   Hey-ho! Peter Quince! Flute, the bellows-mender!
   Snout, the tinker! Starveling! God's my life! Stolen
   hence, and left me asleep! I have had a most rare
   vision. I have had a dream, past the wit of man to say   215
   what dream it was. Man is but an ass, if he go about
   to expound this dream. Methought I was—there
   is no man can tell what. Methought I was and
   methought I had,—but man is but a patched fool if
   he will offer to say what methought I had. The eye of   220
   man hath not heard, the ear of man hath not seen,
   man's hand is not able to taste, his tongue to
   conceive, nor his heart to report, what my dream
   was. I will get Peter Quince to write a ballad of this
   dream. It shall be called "Bottom's Dream"   225
   because it hath no bottom; and I will sing it in the
   latter end of a play, before the Duke. Peradventure,
   to make it the more gracious, I shall sing it at her death.
                        He exits.

Act 4, Scene 2
        Enter QUINCE, FLUTE, SNOUT, and STARVELING

QUINCE Have you sent to Bottom's house? Is he come
   home yet?

STARVELING He cannot be heard of. Out of doubt he
   is transported.

FLUTE If he come not, then the play is marred. It goes   5
   not forward, doth it?

186. overbear: overrule

192. In great solemnity: with great ceremonious pomp

200. Mine own...own: Mine for now, but on which another may lay an earlier claim

216. go about: attempt

219. patched: dressed in motley, the costume a professional fool would wear
220-24. The eye...dream was: *(Bottom's confused recitation of I Corinthians 2:9)*

A MIDSUMMER NIGHT'S DREAM
Act 4. Scene 2

3. Out of doubt: without a doubt
4. transported: carried away by magic

QUINCE It is not possible. You have not a man in all Athens able to discharge Pyramus but he.

FLUTE No, he hath simply the best wit of any handicraft man in Athens.

QUINCE Yea and the best person too, and he is a very paramour for a sweet voice.

FLUTE You must say "paragon." A paramour is, (God bless us), a thing of naught.

Enter SNUG

SNUG Masters, the duke is coming from the temple, and there is two or three lords and ladies more married. If our sport had gone forward, we had all been made men.

FLUTE O, sweet bully Bottom! Thus hath he lost six pence a day during his life. He could not have 'scaped sixpence a day. An the duke had not given him sixpence a day for playing Pyramus, I'll be hanged. He would have deserved it. Sixpence a day in Pyramus, or nothing.

Enter Bottom.

BOTTOM Where are these lads? Where are these hearts?

QUINCE Bottom! O most courageous day! O most happy hour!

BOTTOM Masters, I am to discourse wonders. But ask me not what; for if I tell you, I am no true Athenian. I will tell you every thing, right as it fell out.

QUINCE Let us hear, sweet Bottom.

BOTTOM Not a word of me. All that I will tell you is, that the Duke hath dined. Get your apparel together, good strings to your beards, new ribbons to your pumps. Meet presently at the palace. Every man look o'er his part. For the short and the long is, our play is preferred. In any case, let Thisby have clean linen, and let not him that plays the lion pare his nails, for they shall hang out for the lion's claws. And, most dear actors, eat no onions nor garlic, for we are to utter sweet breath, and I do not doubt but to hear them say, it is a sweet comedy. No more words. Away! Go, away!

They exit.

Act 5, Scene 1

Enter Theseus, Hippolyta, Philostrate, Lords and Attendants.

HIPPOLYTA
'Tis strange my Theseus, that these lovers speak of.

THESEUS
More strange than true. I never may believe
These antique fables, nor these fairy toys.
Lovers and madmen have such seething brains,
Such shaping fantasies, that apprehend
More than cool reason ever comprehends.
The lunatic, the lover, and the poet
Are of imagination all compact.
One sees more devils than vast hell can hold:
That is the madman. The lover, all as frantic,
Sees Helen's beauty in a brow of Egypt.
The poet's eye, in fine frenzy rolling,
Doth glance from heaven to earth, from earth to heaven,

10

15

20

25

30

35

40

45

5

10

---

8. discharge: perform

11. best person: correct appearance

14. thing of naught: an evil thing

17-18. if our sport... men: if our play had been well received, our fortunes would have been made

21. An: if

26. hearts: men of spirit, hearty fellows

31-32. right ... fell out: just as it happened

34. of me: from me

36. strings to your beards: strings to tie on your false beards
37. pumps: fancy shoes
39. preferred: advanced

A MIDSUMMER NIGHT'S DREAM
Act 5. Scene 1

1. that: that which

2. may: can
3. antique fables: myths; **toys:** tales

5. shaping fantasies: creative imaginations; **apprehend:** envision

8. of imagination all compact: entirely made up of imagination
10. all as frantic: just as crazed
11. Helen : Helen of Troy; **a brow of Egypt:** a Gypsy woman

And as imagination bodies forth   15
The forms of things unknown, the poet's pen
Turns them to shapes and gives to airy nothing
A local habitation and a name.
Such tricks hath strong imagination,
That, if it would but apprehend some joy,   20
It comprehends some bringer of that joy.
Or in the night, imagining some fear,
How easy is a bush supposed a bear!

HIPPOLYTA
But all the story of the night told over,
And all their minds transfigured so together,   25
More witnesseth than fancy's images
And grows to something of great constancy,
But, howsoever, strange and admirable.

Enter Lovers: Lysander, Demetrius, Hermia, and Helena.

THESEUS
Here come the lovers, full of joy and mirth.—
Joy, gentle friends! Joy and fresh days of love   30
Accompany your hearts!

LYSANDER   More than to us
Wait in your royal walks, your board, your bed!

THESEUS
Come now; what masques, what dances shall we
    have,   35
To wear away this long age of three hours
Between our after-supper and bedtime?
Where is our usual manager of mirth?
What revels are in hand? Is there no play
To ease the anguish of a torturing hour?   40
Call Philostrate.

PHILOSTRATE *[coming forward]*
                  Here, mighty Theseus.

THESEUS
Say, what abridgement have you for this evening,
What masque, what music? How shall we beguile
The lazy time if not with some delight?   45

PHILOSTRATE *[giving Theseus a paper]*
There is a brief how many sports are ripe.
Make choice of which your Highness will see first.

THESEUS
"The battle with the Centaurs, to be sung
By an Athenian eunuch to the harp."
We'll none of that. That have I told my love   50
In glory of my kinsman Hercules.
"The riot of the tipsy Bacchanals,
Tearing the Thracian singer in their rage."
That is an old device; and it was played
When I from Thebes came last a conqueror.   55
"The thrice-three Muses mourning for the death
Of learning, late deceased in beggary."
That is some satire, keen and critical,
Not sorting with a nuptial ceremony.
"A tedious brief scene of young Pyramus   60
And his love Thisbe; very tragical mirth."
"Merry" and "tragical"? "Tedious" and "brief?"
That is hot ice and wondrous strange snow.
How shall we find the concord of this discord?

PHILOSTRATE
A play there is, my lord, some ten words long,   65
(Which is as brief as I have known a play),
But by ten words, my lord, it is too long,
Which makes it tedious; for in all the play,
There is not one word apt, one player fitted:

25. all … together: their minds all suffering the same delusion
26. More witnesses than fancy's images: accounts for more than the imaginary delusions
27. constancy: consistency
28. howsoever: anyway; **admirable:** worthy of wonder

32. More: more joy
33. Wait: await you

44. beguile: lazily spend

46. brief: listing ; **sports:** diversions

54. device: show

59. sorting with: suitable for, befitting

And tragical, my noble lord, it is. 70
For Pyramus therein doth kill himself.
Which, when I saw rehearsed, I must confess,
Made mine eyes water; but more merry tears
The passion of loud laughter never shed.

THESEUS
What are they that do play it? 75

PHILOSTRATE
Hard-handed men that work in Athens here,
Which never labored in their minds till now,
And now have toiled their unbreathed memories
With this same play, against your nuptial.

THESEUS
And we will hear it. 80

PHILOSTRATE   No, my noble lord,
It is not for you. I have heard it over,
And it is nothing, nothing in the world,
Unless you can find sport in their intents,
Extremely stretched and conned with cruel pain, 85
To do you service.

THESEUS   I will hear that play,
For never anything can be amiss
When simpleness and duty tender it.
Go, bring them in—and take your places, ladies. 90
                    Philostrate exits.

HIPPOLYTA
I love not to see wretchedness o'ercharged
And duty in his service perishing.

THESEUS
Why, gentle sweet, you shall see no such thing.

HIPPOLYTA
He says they can do nothing in this kind.

THESEUS
The kinder we, to give them thanks for nothing. 95
Our sport shall be to take what they mistake;
And what poor duty cannot do, noble respect
Takes it in might, not merit.
Where I have come, great clerks have purposèd
To greet me with premeditated welcomes, 100
Where I have seen them shiver and look pale,
Make periods in the midst of sentences,
Throttle their practiced accent in their fears,
And in conclusion dumbly have broke off,
Not paying me a welcome. Trust me, sweet, 105
Out of this silence yet I picked a welcome;
And in the modesty of fearful duty,
I read as much as from the rattling tongue
Of saucy and audacious eloquence.
Love, therefore, and tongue-tied simplicity 110
In least speak most, to my capacity.

                    Enter Philostrate.
PHILOSTRATE
So please your grace, the Prologue is addressed.

THESEUS
Let him approach.

                    Enter Quince as the Prologue.

QUINCE *as Prologue*
If we offend, it is with our good will.
    That you should think we come not to offend, 115
But with goodwill. To show our simple skill,
    That is the true beginning of our end.

---

78. toiled: exhausted; **unbreathed:** unexercised
79. against: in preparation for

85. extremely stretched: pushed to the breaking point; **conned:** memorized

91. wretchedness: miserable wretches; **o'ercharged:** overburdened
92. duty in...perishing: duty destroying itself trying too hard to perform its function

96. take: accept
97-98. noble respect...merit: a generous review considers the effort not the effect.
99. come: gone; **clerks:** learned men
100. premeditated: previously designed

103. practiced accent: rehearsed line delivery

111. capacity: belief

114-24. If...know: *(For comic effect, this prologue is deliberately mispunctuated.)*

Consider then we come but in despite.
  We do not come, as minding to contest you,
Our true intent is. All for your delight   120
  We are not here. That you should here repent
    you,
The actors are at hand and by their show
You shall know all that you are like to know.
              Prologue exits.

119. minding: intending

THESEUS This fellow doth not stand upon points.   125

125. stand upon points: pays no attention to punctuation
127. stop: period

LYSANDER He hath rid his prologue like a rough colt;
he knows not the stop. A good moral, my lord: it is
not enough to speak, but to speak true.

HIPPOLYTA Indeed he hath played on his prologue like
a child on a recorder; a sound, but not in
government.   130

130-31. in government: controlled

THESEUS His speech, was like a tangled chain—nothing
impaired, but all disordered. Who is next?

      Enter Pyramus (Bottom) and Thisbe (Flute)
      and Wall (Snout) and Moonshine (Starveling)
      and Lion (Snug) and Prologue (Quince).

QUINCE *as Prologue*
Gentles, perchance you wonder at this show.
  But wonder on, till truth make all things plain.   135
This man is Pyramus, if you would know.
  This beauteous lady Thisby is certain.
This man, with lime and roughcast, doth present
  "Wall," that vile Wall which did these lovers
    sunder;   140
And through Wall's chink, poor souls, they are
    content
  To whisper. At the which let no man wonder.
This man, with lantern, dog, and bush of thorn,
  Presenteth "Moonshine," for, if you will know,   145
By moonshine did these lovers think no scorn
  To meet at Ninus' tomb, there, there to woo.
This grisly beast (which "Lion" hight by name)
  The trusty Thisby, coming first by night
Did scare away, or rather did affright;   150
And, as she fled, her mantle she did fall,
  Which Lion vile with bloody mouth did stain.
Anon comes Pyramus, sweet youth and tall,
  And finds his trusty Thisby's mantle slain.
Whereat, with blade, with bloody blameful blade,   155
  He bravely broached is boiling bloody breast.
And Thisby, tarrying in mulberry shade,
  His dagger drew, and died. For all the rest,
Let Lion, Moonshine, Wall, and lovers twain
At large discourse, while here they do remain.   160
      Thisbe, Lion, Moonshine and Prologue exit.

153. tall: brave

156. broached: stabbed

160. At large: in full

THESEUS I wonder if the lion be to speak.

DEMETRIUS No wonder, my lord: one lion may, when
many asses do.

SNOUT *as Wall*
In this same interlude it doth befall
That I, one Snout by name, present a wall;   165
And such a wall as I would have you think,
That had in it a crannied hole or chink,
Through which the lovers, Pyramus and Thisby,
Did whisper often very secretly.
This loam, this roughcast and this stone doth show   170
That I am that same wall; the truth is so.
And this the cranny is, right and sinister,
Through which the fearful lovers are to whisper.

172. right and sinister: right and left

THESEUS Would you desire lime and hair to speak better? 175

DEMETRIUS It is the wittiest partition that ever I heard discourse, my lord.

THESEUS Pyramus draws near the wall: silence!

BOTTOM *as Pyramus*
O grim-looked night! O night with hue so black!
  O night, which ever art when day is not! 180
O night! O night! Alack, alack, alack,
  I fear my Thisby's promise is forgot!
And thou, O wall, O sweet, O lovely wall,
  That stand'st between her father's ground and
    mine, 185
Thou wall, O wall, O sweet and lovely wall,
  Show me thy chink, to blink through with mine
    eyne!
Thanks, courteous wall: Jove shield thee well for
    this! 190
  But what see I? No Thisby do I see.
O wicked wall, through whom I see no bliss,
  Cursed be thy stones for thus deceiving me!

THESEUS The wall, methinks, being sensible, should curse again. 195

BOTTOM No, in truth, sir, he should not. 'Deceiving me' is Thisby's cue. She is to enter now, and I am to spy her through the wall. You shall see it will fall pat as I told you. Yonder she comes.

Enter Flute as Thisbe.

FLUTE *as Thisbe*
O wall, full often hast thou heard my moans 200
  For parting my fair Pyramus and me.
My cherry lips have often kissed thy stones,
  Thy stones with lime and hair knit up in thee.

BOTTOM *as Pyramus*
I see a voice: now will I to the chink,
  To spy an I can hear my Thisbe's face. 205
Thisbe?

FLUTE *as Thisbe*
    My love thou art, my love I think.

BOTTOM *as Pyramus*
Think what thou wilt, I am thy lover's grace,
And, like Limander, am I trusty still.

FLUTE *as Thisbe*
And I like Helen, till the Fates me kill. 210
BOTTOM *as Pyramus*
Not Shafalus to Procrus was so true.

FLUTE *as Thisbe*
As Shafalus to Procrus, I to you.

BOTTOM *as Pyramus*
O kiss me through the hole of this vile wall.

FLUTE *as Thisbe*
I kiss the wall's hole, not your lips at all.

BOTTOM *as Pyramus*
Wilt thou at Ninny's tomb meet me straightway? 215

FLUTE *as Thisbe*
'Tide life, 'tide death, I come without delay.
    Bottom and Flute exit.

SNOUT *as Wall*
Thus have I, Wall, my part discharged so;
And, being done, thus Wall away doth go.
    He exits

174. lime and hair: the materials that make up roughcast

189. Jove shield thee: God reward you

194. being sensible: having senses
195. curse again: return the curse

198-99. fall pat: happen exactly

205. an: if

209. Limander: mispronunication of "Leander," a famous lover

211. Shafalus, Procrus: mispronunciation of Cephalus and Procris, famous tragic lovers

215. Ninny's tomb: i.e., Ninus's tomb
216. 'Tide ... death: come life or death

THESEUS Now is the wall down between the two
    neighbors.   220

DEMETRIUS No remedy, my lord, when walls are so
    willful to hear without warning.

222. to: as to

HIPPOLYTA This is the silliest stuff that ever I heard.

THESEUS The best in this kind are but shadows, and
    the worst are no worse, if imagination amend   225
    them.

224. in this kind: plays; **shadows:** illusions, not real

HIPPOLYTA It must be your imagination then, and not
    theirs.

THESEUS If we imagine no worse of them than they of
    themselves, they may pass for excellent men. Here   230
    come two noble beasts in, a man and a lion.

        Enter Snug as Lion and Starveling as Moonshine.

SNUG *as Lion*
You, ladies, you, whose gentle hearts do fear
    The smallest monstrous mouse that creeps on
        floor,
May now perchance both quake and tremble here,   235
    When lion rough in wildest rage doth roar.
Then know that I, one Snug the joiner, am
A lion fell, nor else no lion's dam;
For, if I should as lion come in strife
Into this place, 'twere pity on my life.   240

238. A lion fell ... dam: neither a fierce lion nor a
lioness in reality

THESEUS A very gentle beast, of a good
    conscience.

DEMETRIUS The very best at a beast, my lord, that e'er
    I saw.

LYSANDER This lion is a very fox for his valor.   245

THESEUS True; and a goose for his discretion.

247. cannot carry: does not exceed

DEMETRIUS Not so, my lord; for his valor cannot carry
    his discretion; and the fox carries the goose.

THESEUS His discretion, I am sure, cannot carry his
    valor; for the goose carries not the fox. It is well.   250
    Leave it to his discretion, and let us listen to the
    Moon.

STARVELING *as Moonshine*
This lanthorn doth the hornèd moon present.

DEMETRIUS He should have worn the horns on his
    head.   255

254-55. horns ... head: an old joke implying he is a
cuckold (that his wife has had an affair)

THESEUS He is no crescent, and his horns are invisible
    within the circumference.

STARVELING *as Moonshine*
This lanthorn doth the hornèd moon present;
    Myself the man i' the moon do seem to be.

THESEUS This is the greatest error of all the rest, the   260
    man should be put into the lanthorn. How is it else
    "the man i' the moon"?

DEMETRIUS He dares not come there for the candle,
    for, you see, it is already in snuff.

263. for the candle: for fear of the candle
264. In snuff: angry

HIPPOLYTA I am aweary of this moon: would he   265
    would change!

THESEUS It appears, by his small light of discretion, that
    he is in the wane; but yet, in courtesy, in all reason,
    we must stay the time.

269. stay: await

LYSANDER Proceed, Moon.   270

STARVELING *as Moonshine* All that I have to say, is,
  to tell you that the lanthorn is the moon; I, the man i' the
  moon; this thornbush, my thornbush; and this dog,
  my dog.

DEMETRIUS Why, all these should be in the lanthorn;   275
  for all these are in the moon. But, silence. Here comes
  Thisbe.

Enter Flute as Thisbe.

FLUTE *as Thisbe*
This is old Ninny's tomb. Where is my love?

SNUG *as Lion*   Oh!
The Lion roars. Thisbe runs off, dropping her mantle.

DEMETRIUS Well roared, Lion.   280

THESEUS Well run, Thisbe.

HIPPOLYTA Well shone, Moon. Truly, the moon shines
  with a good grace.

The Lion worries the mantle.

THESEUS Well moused, Lion.

284. moused: The mantle has been torn or shaken, as a cat with a mouse.

Enter Bottom as Pyramus.

DEMETRIUS And then came Pyramus.   285

Lion exits.

LYSANDER And so the lion vanished.

BOTTOM *as Pyramus*
Sweet Moon, I thank thee for thy sunny beams.
  I thank thee, Moon, for shining now so bright,
For, by thy gracious, golden, glittering gleams,
  I trust to take of truest Thisby sight.—   290
    But stay, O spite!
    But mark, poor knight,
  What dreadful dole is here!

293. dole: sorrow

    Eyes, do you see?
    How can it be?   295
  O dainty duck! O dear!
    Thy mantle good,
    What, stained with blood!
  Approach, ye Furies fell!
    O Fates, come, come,   300
    Cut thread and thrum;
  Quail, crush, conclude, and quell!

299. Furies: three beings of classical mythological who punished those who offended against natural and moral laws; **fell:** fierce, deadly
300. Fates: three beings of classical mythology who spun the thread of each human's destiny, determined its length, and cut it to end the human's life.
301. thrum: the unwoven end of thread in fabric
302. quell: kill

THESEUS This passion, and the death of a dear friend,
  would go near to make a man look sad.

HIPPOLYTA Beshrew my heart, but I pity the man.   305

303. passion: staging of great sorrow
305. Beshrew: curse
306. wherefore: why
307. deflowered: a malapropism (verbal confusion) for "devoured"

BOTTOM *as Pyramus*
O wherefore, Nature, didst thou lions frame,
Since lion vile hath here deflowered my dear,
Which is—no, no—which was the fairest dame
That lived, that loved, that liked, that looked with
  cheer.   310
    Come, tears, confound!
    Out, sword, and wound!
  The pap of Pyramus;
    Ay, that left pap,
    Where heart doth hop.   315

311. confound: destroy

313. pap: breast, nipple

Pyramus stabs himself
  Thus die I, thus, thus, thus.
    Now am I dead,
    Now am I fled;
  My soul is in the sky.
    Tongue, lose thy light!   320

Moon take thy flight!
Moonshine exits.
Now die, die, die, die, die.
Pyramus falls.

DEMETRIUS No die, but an ace, for him, for he is but
one.

LYSANDER Less than an ace, man, for he is dead, he is   325
nothing.

THESEUS With the help of a surgeon he might yet recover,
and prove an ass.

HIPPOLYTA How chance Moonshine is gone before
Thisbe comes back and finds her lover?

Enter Thisbe as Flute.

THESEUS She will find him by starlight.
Here she comes; and her passion ends the play.

HIPPOLYTA Methinks she should not use a long one for
such a Pyramus: I hope she will be brief.

DEMETRIUS A mote will turn the balance, which   335
Pyramus, which Thisbe, is the better; he for a man,
God warrant us; she for a woman, God bless us.

LYSANDER She hath spied him already with those
sweet eyes.

DEMETRIUS And thus she means, videlicet:—   340

FLUTE *as Thisbe*
Asleep, my love?
What, dead, my dove?
O Pyramus, arise!
Speak, speak. Quite dumb?
Dead, dead? A tomb   345
Must cover thy sweet eyes.
These lily lips,
This cherry nose,
These yellow cowslip cheeks
Are gone, are gone!   350
Lovers, make moan;
His eyes were green as leeks.
O Sisters Three,
Come, come to me
With hands as pale as milk.   355
Lay them in gore,
Since you have shore
With shears his thread of silk.
Tongue, not a word!
Come, trusty sword,   360
Come, blade, my breast imbrue!
Thisbe stabs herself.
And, farewell, friends.
Thus Thisby ends.
Adieu, adieu, adieu.
Thisbe falls.

THESEUS Moonshine and Lion are left to bury the   365
dead.

DEMETRIUS Ay, and Wall too.
Bottom and Flute arise.

BOTTOM No assure you; the wall is down that
parted their fathers. Will it please you to see the
Epilogue, or to hear a Bergomask dance between   370
two of our company?

THESEUS No epilogue, I pray you; for your play needs
no excuse. Never excuse. For when the players are
all dead, there needs none to be blamed. Marry, if

323. die: one of a pair of dice

340. means: moans, laments; **videlicet:** as follows

353. Sisters Three: the Fates *(see line 300)*

357. shore: shorn, cut

361. imbrue: stain or drench (with blood)

370. Bergomask dance: a rustic, clownish dance

he that writ it had played Pyramus and hanged   375
himself in Thisbe's garter, it would have been a fine
tragedy; and so it is, truly; and very notably
discharged. But come, your Bergomask. Let your
epilogue alone.

Dance, and the players exit.

The iron tongue of midnight hath told twelve.   380
Lovers, to bed! 'Tis almost fairy time.
I fear we shall outsleep the coming morn
As much as we this night have overwatched.
This palpable-gross play hath well beguiled
The heavy gait of night. Sweet friends, to bed.   385
A fortnight hold we this solemnity
In nightly revels and new jollity.
They exit.
Enter Robin Goodfellow.

ROBIN
Now the hungry lion roars,
  And the wolf behowls the moon,
Whilst the heavy plowman snores,   390
  All with weary task fordone.
Now the wasted brands do glow,
  Whilst the screech-owl, screeching loud,
Puts the wretch that lies in woe
  In remembrance of a shroud.   395
Now it is the time of night
  That the graves, all gaping wide,
Every one lets forth his sprite,
  In the church-way paths to glide.
And we fairies, that do run   400
  By the triple Hecate's team,
From the presence of the sun,
  Following darkness like a dream,
Now are frolic. Not a mouse
Shall disturb this hallowed house.   405
I am sent with broom before,
To sweep the dust behind the door.

Enter Oberon and Titania, King and Queen of Fairies,
with all their train.

OBERON
Through the house give gathering light,
  By the dead and drowsy fire.
Every elf and fairy sprite,   410
  Hop as light as bird from brier,
And this ditty, after me,
Sing, and dance it trippingly.

TITANIA
First, rehearse your song by rote,
To each word a warbling note.   415
Hand in hand, with fairy grace,
Will we sing, and bless this place.

Oberon leads the Fairies in song and dance.

OBERON
Now, until the break of day,
Through this house each fairy stray.
To the best bride-bed will we,   420
Which by us shall blessèd be;
And the issue there create
Ever shall be fortunate.
So shall all the couples three
Ever true in loving be,   425
And the blots of Nature's hand
Shall not in their issue stand.

380. iron tongue of midnight: the clapper of the midnight bell

383. overwatched: stayed awake
384. palpable-gross: obviously dim-witted

391. fordone: exhausted
392. wasted brands: burned-up logs

401. triple Hecate's team: Hecate ruled in three aspects: Luna, the moon in heaven; Diana on earth; and Proserpina in hell.
404. frolic: merry

422. there create: created there

426. the blots of Nature's hand: deformities
427. issue: offspring, children

Never mole, hare lip, nor scar,
Nor mark prodigious, such as are
Despisèd in nativity,   430
Shall upon their children be.
With this field-dew consecrate,
Every fairy take his gait,
And each several chamber bless,
Through this palace, with sweet peace.   435   **434. several:** individual
And the owner of it blest,
Ever shall in safety rest.
Trip away; make no stay.
Meet me all by break of day.

                    All but Robin exit.

ROBIN
If we shadows have offended,   440   **440. shadows:** actors
Think but this, and all is mended:
That you have but slumbered here
While these visions did appear.
And this weak and idle theme,
No more yielding but a dream,   445
Gentles, do not reprehend.
If you pardon, we will mend.
And, as I am an honest Puck,
If we have unearnèd luck
Now to 'scape the serpent's tongue,   450   **450. serpent's tongue:** hisses (from the audience)
We will make amends ere long;
Else the Puck a liar call.
So, good night unto you all.
Give me your hands, if we be friends,   **454. Give me your hands:** applaud
And Robin shall restore amends.   455
                    He exits.

REVENGE TRAGEDIES

Revenge tragedies were popular in the Elizabethan and Jacobean (King James) eras.
The best-known is Shakespeare's **Hamlet**, although some elements of revenge tragedy may be
found in **Titus Andronicus**, **Julius Caesar** and **Macbeth**.

Elements of Revenge Tragedy include:

A secret murder, often of a "good" ruler by an "evil" successor;

An earthly return by the ghost of the victim to a relative (often father by son, or vice versa);

A revenge plot by a close relative of the victim;

A delay or hesitation by the avenger;

A period of insanity (real or imaginary) by the avenger or another character;

The intrigue (perhaps political) between murderer and avenger, often a scheming villain;

One or more philosophical soliloquys ("To be, or not to be" in **Hamlet**);

The sensational use of horror;

A suicide and/or sensational use of violence, with an ever-increasing body count;

A climactic scene that greatly reduces the number of characters, usually including the avenger.

THE RESTORATION THEATRE

Queen Elizabeth I died in 1603, and was succeeded by King James VI of Scotland, who became **King James I** of England. He was succeeded by his son, **King Charles I**, in 1625. These three monarchs had supported the theatre.

The English Civil War (1641–1651) was a three-part conflict between Parliamentarians and Royalists that led to the trial and execution of Charles I, the exile of his son, Charles II. The monarchy was replaced first with the **Commonwealth** (1649–53), and then the **Protectorate** (1653–59) under the rule of Oliver Cromwell. During the **Interregnum** ("between kings"), theatre was outlawed. Theatre buildings were closed (or dismantled), and scripts and costumes were destroyed.

In 1660, Parliament invited **Charles II**, who had been living in the court of theatre-loving Louis XIV of France, to reclaim the English throne. With the monarchy "restored," theatres opened immediately. The Drury Lane and Covent Gardens were among the first officially licensed theatres.

Restoration Theatre rebelled against Puritanic ideals and was characterized by witty/bawdy dialogue and the relaxed morality/sexual behavior of the aristocracy. Men and boys were forbidden to play female roles, and women were allowed to perform on stage. (Two of King Charles II's mistresses were actresses Nell Gywn and Moll Davies.)

Notable Restoration playwrights and comedies include:

John Dryden (1631-1700), *Marriage-a-la-Mode* (1672)
William Wycherley (c. 1640-1715), *The Country Wife* (1675)
George Etherege (c. 1635-1692), *The Man of Mode* (1676)
William Congreve (1670-1729), *The Way of the World* (1700)

By the early 1700s these amoral plays had overstepped public decency and fell out of favor as the Neo-Classical idea of teaching morals became the accepted style.

THE BAROQUE ERA (1600-1750)

While religious conflicts raged throughout Europe, the Catholic Counter-Reformation encouraged the Baroque art style, which brought an opulence to the visual and performing arts. ("**More** is more.") "Classical" music began. Architecture relied on monumental size and elaborate decorations. Royal courts in Europe (especially Louis XIV of France) used the style to prove their wealth and power.

The term **Theatrum Mundi** ("the world is a stage") was created as new theatre technology and scenery techniques using ropes and pulleys were used. Elaborately-plotted plays would become less popular in favor of operas, which would combine several art forms into a unified whole.

Opera has all of its text set to music and is sung to orchestra accompaniment by classically trained singers. Opera is characterized by elaborate costuming, scenery and choreography. Opera originated in Italy. The first known opera was "Dafne" in 1593.

Operetta is "light opera" in terms of music and subject matters less serious than operas. Operetta also features classically trained singers.

[In contemporary usage, **Musical Theatre** combines spoken dialogue with songs and dances that advance the plot. Musicals use actors who sing, but not usually trained in an operatic style. Not all musicals are comedies.]

VOCABULARY OF THE THEATRE

ACT (verb) To perform in a play. (noun) The major division, or separation, in a play, musical, or opera. Most modern plays are divided into two acts, sometimes three. Not all act divisions have intermissions.

ACTING AREA One of the nine areas into which the stage space is divided in order to accommodate blocking and movement, e.g. Downstage Right (DR), Downstage Center (DC), Downstage Left (DL), Right (R), Center (C), Left (L), Upstage Right (UR), Upstage Center (UC), Upstage Left (UL). **In the United States, the stage directions left and right always refer to the actor's left and right.**

ACT CURTAIN The main curtain directly behind the grand drape which can move vertically or horizontally to conceal scenery from an audience before, during, or after a production. If the act curtain raises vertically, it is a Fly Curtain; if it is drawn horizontally, it is a Draw Curtain.

ACTION The psychological, emotional, and physical happenings that convey the meaning and story of a dramatic work. *See Tone.*

ACTOR/AUDIENCE RELATIONSHIP An immediate and personal exchange which gives live theatre its special quality.

ADLIB Improvised lines of dialogue which are not part of the dramatist's script. Often said if an actor "goes up" on a line or in an emergency.

ALLEGORY A work which moves on different levels of interpretation and employs literal, veiled, or hidden meanings, e.g. in *Everyman* [c. 1500], the character seeks aid from figures called Good Deeds, Kindred, Death, Beauty, etc. in order to talk about the real world. Symbolists present the "real world" in order to reveal a "higher" eternal world of which the symbol is a part. A narrative where abstractions are made concrete.

ANACHRONISM Placing a person, event, or object outside of its proper time; e.g. the onstage use of an electric light in a Greek tragedy.

APRON The stage space extending front of the proscenium arch or forward of the curtain line. Also called the forestage.

ASIDE A remark or speech in a drama made by a character (heard by the spectator) while in the presence of others, assumed not to be heard by other characters present, and directed at the audience. An Elizabethan convention used later in Melodrama. The aside had scattered use in the 20th century, e.g. O'Neill's *Strange Interlude*.

AT RISE A technical term used to describe what is happening on stage at the moment the curtain opens or the first scene is illuminated.

ATMOSPHERE The pervading mood in a theatrical work partially created by set, lights, language and action; it establishes the expectations of the spectators' attitude: the "brooding" atmosphere in an O'Neill play.

AUDITIONS The reading session at which actors present a prepared monologue or do a "cold" reading to determine their suitability for a particular role. For musicals, actors must do a musical, dramatic, and dance audition to determine suitability for a role. In the professional theatre, actors have Equity Principal Interviews (EPIs), an initial interview/screening, and Equity Principal Auditions (EPAs), at which the auditors screen actors for principal roles.

BACKSTAGE The stage area behind the front curtain and away from the actual playing area on stage. Areas include dressing rooms, green room, offstage, and wings.

BLACKOUT The sudden switching-off of all lights on stage.

BLANK VERSE A succession of unrhymed poetic lines in iambic pentameter. Lines of ten syllables, with accents on the 2nd, 4th, 6th, 8th, and 10th in a rising rhythm. Introduced into English poetry by the Earl of Surrey in the 16th century, blank verse became the most frequent meter for verse or poetic drama in English after Christopher Marlowe.

BLOCKING A director's organization of the actors' movement on stage in order to create effective compositional pictures with respect to each other and the surrounding stage space.

BOOK (noun) The spoken text (dialogue) of a musical, often referred to as the libretto. (verb) To schedule work for artists and productions.

CATHARSIS A purifying of one's emotions through the effect of art because of pity or fear while watching a tragic drama; a relief, or discharge of relief, of painful emotions as in love stories when the protagonist dies. From a Greek word translated as "purgation" employed by Aristotle when defining tragedy. *See Pathos and Empathy.*

CHARACTER A person in a dramatic work; the personalities of the figures in the stories. The playwright can achieve character through speeches, actions, thoughts, emotions, and other's opinions. The central character in a play is called the **protagonist** and the individual, thing or force opposing or rivaling the protagonist is called the **antagonist**.

CHARACTERIZATION The technique used by actors to bring to life the physical and inner-life qualities of a character in a play. The art by which an author imbues a character with life, accomplished through the reactions of other characters, the character's speech and actions, what they do, and what the author says about them. Also, the physical, sociological, psychological, and moral attributes of a character.

CHOREOGRAPHER The director of the dance sequences in musicals. For directors who don't stage musical numbers, a choreographer will "stage" or create movement for the musical numbers, referred to as musical staging. In 1970, the Director/Choreographer entered the Broadway scene moving the American musical theatre in the direction Jerome Robbins attempted in 1959 with *West Side Story*. Broadway's greatest choreographers were Agnes DeMille, Michael Kidd, Jerome Robbins, Gower Champion, Michael Bennett, and Bob Fosse.

CHORUS In Greek drama, a group of actors who sang, chanted, spoke, or moved in unison either adding to the action or commenting upon it. In modern use, a group of singer/dancers in musicals, operettas, ballets, and operas, who perform as a group rather than as an individual.

CLICHE An expression used so often that it is drained of meaning.

COMIC RELIEF The use of humorous speeches and incidents in the course of serious or tragic action to relieve tension permitting the emotional surge to be later intensified.

COMPANY The group of actors, staff, and crew permanently attached to a show.

CONVENTION An accepted lie in the theatre; an agreed upon way of doing something which, though different from actuality, is willingly accepted by the audience. Also, a stock character such as the drunken porter in *Macbeth*.

COSTUME PIECE A theatrical work written outside the lifespan of its author, e.g. *A Man For All Seasons* by Robert Bolt, *Murder In The Cathedral* by T. S. Eliot's, *Man of LaMancha* by Leigh and Wasserstein, and *1776* by Stone and Edwards. *See Period Piece.*

CREW(S) A team of individuals responsible for assisting with the construction and often the running of all technical elements during a production, e.g. Running crews for scenery, light crew for running a follow spot, light board, costume crew for wardrobe changes during performances, prop crew, etc. Also known as stage crew.

CRISIS A turning point; a decisive moment of instability or indecision for a character. Every crisis must have a climax.

CUE A prearranged signal to or from an actor or stagehand which can be visual, auditory, or musical that indicates "go cues" for dialogue, light or set changes, follow spots, songs, or lines of dialogue during a performance of a play or musical.

CURTAIN CALL A custom at least as old as Roman theatre. Also called "bows", the cast shows their respect for the audience by bowing while the audience shows their appreciation for the cast by applauding.

CYCLORAMA A large, expansive cloth or muslin usually an off-white color or pale blue that can be used for a "sky" backing for scenery or projections. In some theatres, it is a plaster wall or similar material that is the back wall of a theatre. Usually shortened to "cyc".

DIALECT The speech pattern characteristic of a specific region or class. Also, the variations in usage of the same language by different groups of people, caused by geographical, cultural, and ethnic differences.

DIALOGUE The conversation between two or more characters in a dramatic work that advances the play's action.

DICTION A writer's choice and use of words. The clear and precise vocal articulation of the author's words in a dramatic production.

DIRECTOR   The manager of a troupe; the Greeks called him *didachylus*; the Romans called him *manager of a troupe*; in Medieval times he was referred to as *maitre de Jeu* or *metteur de Scene*; during the Renaissance he was called *architech* or *leader of the troupe*; in the 18th- and 19th centuries he was an *actor-manager*; in early 20th century, he was a *regisseur*; and in England he was called the *producer*. In 1874, the Duke of Saxe-Meiningen originated the "ensemble" method of playing in Berlin. He devised a system in which a single mind brought scenery, costume, lighting, and acting into one artistic whole. Adolphe Appia and Gordon Craig soon followed. The principal function of a director is to unify and correlate elements of a theatrical production in a fashion that will enable him or her to interpret the essential meaning of the script in order to project a single image or point of view to the audience. S/he is an interpretive artist during collaboration with the dramatists, actors, and designers. The finest directors are intelligent, sensitive, imaginative, have showmanship, a sense of rhythm, humor, and tact, leadership qualities, organizations skills, good taste and a sure sense of style; energy, talent, dedication, training in history, dramatic theory, period styles, technical elements, knowledge of acting and problems of actors, criteria for knowing good from bad acting, psychology, and mostly patience.

DIRECT ADDRESS   A character turns from the world of the stage and speaks directly to the audience, e.g. the opening and closing "Ballad of Sweeney Todd" from the Stephen Sondheim's Musical Thriller, *Sweeney Todd: The Demon Barber of Fleet Street*, or Tom's speeches in Tennessee Williams', *The Glass Menagerie*.

DOUBLING   Assigning one actor to play two or more roles in the same play.

DOWNSTAGE   The front-half of the stage closest to the audience or any part of the stage considered closer to the audience. An actor always "comes" downstage. The origin of the term dates to raked stages from front to back and actors had to literally walk "down" the stage towards the audience. *See Upstage.*

DRESS THE STAGE   A directorial instruction to an actor or actors requesting them to make minor shifts in positions which improve focus and composition, and ensure maximum visibility to an audience.

DROP   A large piece of painted canvas or muslin, fastened to battens at the top and bottom, hung in the flies in a specific position, or serves as a backdrop for a scene in a play or musical. Exterior sets use backdrops to depict exotic, pastoral, or any painted landscape.

EMPATHY   The audience sympathizes with the character(s) on stage and forms a bond, causing one to feel remorse or joy when the characters do. Also, the experience of mentally entering into the feelings, emotions, and spirit of the actor's characterization.

ENTR'ACTE   The overture that opens the second act of a musical.

ENTRANCE   The arrival on stage of an actor into a scene.

EPILOGUE   An appendix to a play, a short concluding scene at the end of a play, or concluding direct address such as Puck's closing speech in *A Midsummer Night's Dream,* Dromio's epilogue at the conclusion of *A Comedy Of Errors*, or the funeral scene in *Death Of A Salesman*.

EXIT   The leaving of the stage by an actor.

EXTRA(S)   Characters in a play, movie, or television with no lines and who are never important as individuals. Also referred to as supernumeraries or "supers." *See Walk-ons.*

FLASHBACK An abrupt movement from present to past and back again in a scene within a play. Also, scenes or incidents in a play that happen prior to the opening scene and interrupt the chronological order of the action. Flashbacks and foreshadowing enhance the suspense of the plot.

FLAT A single piece of scenery which used to be made of stretched canvas over wood, now often replaced by luan, and used with other similar pieces to form all or part of a setting.

FORESHADOWING The technique of dropping hints or suggestions that lead the audience to anticipate subsequent events or situations.

FOURTH WALL The imaginary or open side of the stage that faces the audience and allows them to view the play.

FRENCH SCENE The entrance or exit of a new character in a scene changing the groups' composition. Directors often break down lengthy scenes into French Scenes for rehearsal purposes.

FRONT OF HOUSE The expression used for the area of a theatre designated specifically for an audience as opposed to the stage and backstage areas. Often it is referred to as just the "house."

GIVEN CIRCUMSTANCES A term from the "method" approach to acting which define the world of the play; i.e. the character's age, social status, health, or any circumstance over which an actor/character has no control.

GREENROOM A backstage lounge area for actors before, during, and after a show.

HISTORICAL PLAY/HISTORICAL DRAMA A about an historical figure that dealt with the major issues of public welfare and had a nationalistic tone. Shakespeare was a major writer of the historical drama.

HUMOR A technique in writing designed to produce laughter or amusement often through emphasis on life's ludicrous or incongruous elements.

IRONY A literary device contrasting appearances and reality. Also, a discrepancy between what is said and what is actually meant, or between what is expected to happen and what actually occurs.

JUXTAPOSITION Intentionally placing two speeches, characters, or incidents side by side for dramatic effect.

LYRIC(S) A compressed poetic treatment of a single subject, candidly expressing personal emotion. Usually written to be sung as in musical theatre.

MAKEUP Cosmetics or applications used by actors to alter their appearance. Straight makeup heightens the appearance of an actor. Character makeup makes an actor look different for his or her actual appearance.

MANUSCRIPT The unpublished version of a dramatic script. Originally a hand written version written by the author or a copy made by a scribe. More recently, it is typed or printed electronically. Often, it has author's and editor's corrections and is cherished as it exists to determine what the author actually intended. There are no extant manuscripts of Shakespeare's plays.

MASK (noun) A facial covering used in Greek plays. (verb) To hide lights, scenery or actors from an audience, the view of lights, scenery, actors.

MASKING A piece of scenery set in a way that prevents spectators from seeing any part of the backstage area during a performance. *See Sightlines.*

MONOLOGUE A speech delivered by one character in a play which may be heard but not interrupted by others in his/her presence; or a speech performed by a single actor alone on stage. *See Soliloquy.*

MOTIVATION The inner drive, purpose, reason, impulse, or intention which makes a character think, act, or react in a certain way.

OBJECTIVE What a protagonist desires most. This strong want, need and desire of the central character becomes the focal point of a play.

OBLIGATORY SCENE In tragedy, the critical final confrontation between the protagonist and the antagonist in which the protagonist wins or loses; a highly emotional moment late in the play, and is followed shortly thereafter by the climax.

OBSTACLE Something that delays, prevents, or obstructs the protagonist in a play, creating conflict and complication.

OFFSTAGE A designated area of the stage, usually in the wings, or backstage and out of the view of an audience. Onstage is in view of the audience. *See Sightlines*

OPEN A term directed towards actors during the rehearsal process requesting him or her to "open up to," or turn more towards the audience.

ORCHESTRA Ground-floor seating in theatres with a balcony. Certain theatres referred to seating arrangements as: Orchestra Section, First Balcony, Second Balcony, or interchanged the phrase balcony for Mezzanine. Also, a group of musicians that accompany musical productions usually placed front and/or below the apron; in some productions, the orchestra can be backstage or onstage, e.g. *The Fantasticks* and *Chicago.*

PANTOMIME Originally a Roman entertainment with a sung narrative by a chorus while a story is performed by dancers. A pantomime is an illustration of a story that depends upon depicted objects, actions, situations. The communication expressed between individuals through movement and gesture remain the essence of the art.

PARABLE A story answering a question or pointing out a moral. The play *Doubt* is subtitled "A Parable."

PARADOX A statement which appears self-contradictory but which reveals an unexpected truth. Paradox sometimes takes the form of an oxymoron; e.g. the phrase, "wild civility" or "the silence is deafening."

PATHOS The quality that evokes pity. Pathetic suffering is experienced by innocent women and children; tragic suffering is experienced by persons who act, struggle, and are in some measure responsible for their sufferings; e.g. Aeschylus' *The Suppliants.*

PERFORMANCE ART A 1980s form of experimental theatre that combines dance, film, and video, and other visual arts with theatre. The director, rather than a playwright, supplies the vision of the production and uses actors as acrobats and dancers rather than characters to form tableaus that precisely fit into the visual and choreographic scheme of the production. Also, includes storytelling and one-person performances.

PERIOD PIECE A theatrical work occurring during the lifespan of its author. The presentation (on stage) of a drama from a former age. e.g. Shakespeare, Marlowe, Moliere, Wilde, etc. *See Costume Piece.*

PLAY (noun) A form of literature written by a playwright that almost always consists of scripted dialogue between characters. The word is also used for activities normally associated with pleasure and enjoyment. English is not the only language that uses the double meaning of "play" as both a game and a theatre production: The French word "*jeu*", the German word "*spiel*" and the Latin word "*ludi*" all refer to both games and a theatrical event.

PRESENTATIONAL THEATRE acknowledges the presence of an audience. There is little illusion in acting, and staging is unrealistic (as opposed to realistic, naturalistic, or representational theatre.) e.g. in Wilder's *Our Town*, a drugstore counter consisted of a board over two chairs. There is frequent direct address to audience, soliloquy, and asides. Musicals and Balletsare presentational, and sometimes referred to as "theatrical staging". Virtually all drama before the 19th century was highly presentational. *Compare Representational Staging.*

PRODUCER On Broadway, the producer is responsible for the business aspects of the production, but also hires (and can fire) the artistic and production staff. In Great Britain, the title "producer" is often synonymous with the work of an American director.

PROLOGUE In Greek plays, the Prologus was the first scene which revealed exposition; Elizabethan prologues summarized the plot as in *Romeo and Juliet.* In the late 17th century, the prologue was an independent verse spoken before the play began. A prologue can also be an actor who speaks the piece described above. Also, a scene or speech that precedes the main action of a play or musical.

PROMPT BOOK A complete production record maintained by the stage manager which notes everything from original blocking notes to light and sound cues, rehearsal and production schedules, director notes, costume plots, floor plans, etc.

PROPERTIES or PROPS   Objects used on the stage, other than scenery and costumes. Usually categorized into Set (trees, furniture) Costume (parasols), Hand/ Personal props (anything from a cup to a cane), and Trim props which are articles that add to the decor of the set; e.g. pictures, mirrors, curtains, etc.

PROPERTY TABLE Usually placed directly offstage right and/or left or at a location easily accessible to the actors.

PROSCENIUM (ARCH) The picture frame or frame of the proscenium (invisible fourth wall).

PUN A play on words based on a similarity of sound between two words with different meanings.

RAKE (or "raked stage") The positioning of stage floor (and scenery) on a slant or angle. The terms "upstage" and "downstage" come from stages that had a stage floor sloping upward away from the audience.

REALISM Creating the illusion of reality or the illusion of life on stage. In the late 19th century, Realism revolted against Romanticism and sentimentality. Major proponents were Ibsen, Chekhov and Strindberg.

REHEARSAL The preparation by a cast and its director towards a finished production.

REPERTOIRE A catalogue or "canon" of authored works mastered by an individual artist or institution, e.g.. a regional theatre that has presented the entire repertoire of Shakespeare's works.

REPERTORY The plays produced by a theatre company available for production at any time.

REPRESENTATIONAL STAGING The characters use illusionary staging by its director which acknowledges the presence of the illusionary fourth wall; the presentation is played for an audience rather than to an audience. *See Presentational Theatre.*

REVIEWER A journalist employed by a newspaper to cover the who, what, when, and where of a theatre production. A reviewer's principal task is to write a capsule synopsis of the plot and audience response, and supply a production photo, and "if you go" facts. *See Theatre Critic.*

ROTATING REPERTORY Different plays are performed on alternate nights by a resident acting company rather than present a single play performed nightly. The Asolo Theatre in Sarasota is one of the few rotating repertory companies in the United States.

ROYALTIES The fees paid to a playwright, lyricist, librettist, or composer (and their agents) for production rights to publicly perform their work.

RUN THROUGH Often written as "Run-thru", it is a rehearsal term meaning to perform an entire scene or act without interruption.

SCENE A smaller unit of an act; can be a shift of locale, time, actor, or group of actors. Also, the location of a play's action or stage setting. *See French Scene.*

SCRIM A thin, open-weave fabric nearly transparent when lit from behind and opaque when lit from the front. There are also painted scrims.

SCRIPT The written text of a play or other type of theatrical presentation. *See Book.*

SET The scenery constructed for a theatrical performance.

SETTING The time (historical period), place (geographical location), socioeconomic background, action, time period (days, weeks, months), cultural environment, and other elements which form the physical background of a dramatic work, and is often a significant element of the play's atmosphere, theme, and tone.

SIGHT LINES The line of sight from any side of the house to the top of the balcony that determines the size and playing area of the stage visible to the spectator.

SLAPSTICK A type of comic business which relies on violent physical sight gags for its humor.

SOLILOQUY A dramatic speech spoken (or sung) by a character to himself rather than to another character, reflecting the character's thoughts. Also, a solitary character speaks (or sings) to an audience, expressing in words (or lyrics), a hidden thought or thoughts that reveal necessary information about him/herself or other characters. A widely used convention in Elizabethan drama and melodrama, e.g. Hamlet's speech "To be, or not to be" or Billy Bigelow's "Soliloquy" from *Carousel. See Monologue.*

SPECIAL A lighting instrument focused on an important individual or area where emphatic action takes place. Specials provide added illumination to specified areas of a set.

S.R.O. Abbreviation or "Standing Room Only" indicating a sold out theatrical performance.

STAGE A platform or space for theatrical performances.

STAGE BUSINESS Physical action by an actor in a play, consisting of anything from lighting a cigarette to making a bed to poisoning a drink, etc. Stock comic bits ("schtick") are more often used in comedy or farce.

STOCK CHARACTER A conventional character type, or stereotype, often anticipated by the spectator as belonging to a particular group. *See Convention.*

STRIKE The term for tearing down a set after the final performance. Also, the term used by a stage manager to the crew during a performance to clear the existing set. e.g. "strike the desk."

STYLE A manner in which art is executed in the characteristic of an individual, time, literary writing, or a place. A mode of expression. The best style matches ideas to the quality of language. Style is felt by an individual and is a result of the creative process, making it difficult to describe or dissect. In verbal terms, people come to recognize art, a dramatic line, or musical composition by the style (signature) of its creator, e.g. Shakespeare, Gershwin, Sondheim, Monet, or Debussy.

SUBTEXT A term from the "method" school of acting for text assumed to be hidden underneath the surface of the text. That which is implied but never stated; the soul of language. Actors are expected to discover and communicate the character's unspoken but felt life.

TABLEAU A "freeze" on stage by all characters that most often paints a portrait, used for numerous theatrical effects.

TECHNICIANS Personnel who perform the necessary functions of the technical elements of a play. e.g. carpenters and technical crews, often referred to as "techies."

THEATRE The physical plant or building which houses theatrical performances. Its components include the stage, dressing rooms, backstage areas, fly space, orchestra pit, orchestra section for audience seating, lobby, and box office areas. Also, the profession which employs live performances before live audiences. [The Oxford Dictionary lists the spelling of theater as a U.S. variation. The etymology of the word shows us that the spelling "theatre" is actually closer in spelling to its Greek (theatron), Latin (theatrum), and Middle English (theatre) origins, and remains the accepted and accurate spelling used throughout the world.]

THEATRE CRITIC An individual who observes the piece and brings his/her scholarship, background, observation, and analysis to bear on the production as a whole. Matthew Arnold said, "Criticism is analysis and evaluation, not opinion." *Compare Reviewer*

THESPIAN Another word for actor, named after Thespis, the first Greek actor.

TONE A literary characteristic designating the attitudes of the author toward his reader, subject, characters, and audience by the way language is used. Tone generally is categorized by "serious", "angry", "joyful", "pious", "poetic", "satirical", etc.

TRAGIC FLAW   In tragedy, the inability of the protagonist to realize his chief weakness causing a vulnerability which intensifies in time of stress. Originated from Greek drama, but can be applied to modern analysis.

TRAP   A large opening in a stage floor used for theatrical effects or entrances and exits by actors, or scenic effects from below the stage. Most professional theatres have stage floors that facilitate a trap in any portion of the stage.

TRILOGY   A unit of three works. The Greeks presented three tragedies at a time; i.e. those that had an internal unity. The only extant example of a Greek Trilogy is Aeschylus', *Orestia* (458 B.C.). Modern trilogies include O'Neill's *Mourning Becomes Electra* (1931), Bock & Hamick's *The Apple Tree, a Musical Trilogy* and Ayckbourn's *The Norman Conquests* (1973).

TYPE CASTING   The hiring (casting) of an actor for a role because of his/her natural appearance, voice, or personality.

UNDERSTUDY   An actor who rehearses a major role but performs the role only if the actor who usually plays the role is unable.

UPSTAGE   The part of the stage farthest from the audience or any part of the stage considered in relation to something further from the audience. To "go upstage" (vs. "come downstage") means to move away from the audience towards the back wall of the theatre. The origin of the term dates to raked stages from front to back and actors had to literally walk "up" the stage towards the back wall. *See Downstage.*

VIGNETTE   A literary sketch having charm and delicacy. Also, a short "sketch" from musical or dramatic works.

WALK-ON   An actor who has no speaking lines but is seen. *See Extra(s).*

WINGS   Areas offstage right and offstage left where actors wait to make their entrance into a scene. Also, narrow standing pieces of scenery which are mounted parallel to the proscenium, which form the sides of a setting.

WIT   A superior intellectual knowledge or insight, usually conveyed with clever humor in verbal expressions, e.g. Oscar Wilde, Noel Coward, Cole Porter and Dorothy Parker, among others.